DISCOVERING

THE I

IN CHRIST

"The more you begin to understand who you are, the less others understand who you are."

-Toks Akinsanmi

Dear SKim,

May God lift you up in every area of your life and cause you to continue to discover yourself in Christ -

5/13/17

One of the many goals of this book is to help you discover who you are in Christ by sharing my spiritual journey and through this reveal how the life of Jesus here on earth is still relevant to you today.

I hope that you will be able to see yourself in the big picture of God's plan through Christ and the Holy Spirit.

I pray that you will be able to see how the life of Jesus here on earth can give a new meaning to your existence and bring about a fulfilled and victorious life.

God was light years ahead of the world when He decided that He would send His Son, Jesus to be crucified on a cross and later resurrected by the Holy Spirit in order for us to walk in authority from our new identity as *sons and daughters of God.*

DISCOVERING
THE I
IN CHRIST

"The more you begin to understand who you are, the less others understand who you are."

TOKS AKINSANMI

INSPIREDSCRIPTS

Discovering The I in ChrIst
Copyright © 2017 by Toks Akinsanmi
All rights reserved.

Unless otherwise stated, all scripture quotations are from the King James Authorized Version of the Bible.

Published in the USA by Inspired Scripts
www.inspiredscripts.org

ISBN: 978-1546393436

Cover and interior design by Ladak Creative Concepts
www.ladakcreativeconcepts.com

All rights reserved. This book is protected by the copyright laws of the United States of America. This book may not be copied or reprinted for commercial gain or profit. The use of short quotations or occasional page copying for personal or group study is permitted and encouraged with credit to the author. Permission for other uses will be granted upon request. All permission requests should be emailed with Subject: Permissions Coordinator to *info@inspiredscripts.org*.

Printed in the United States of America

DEDICATION

To all those who earnestly seek the true meaning of their existence and eagerly desire to begin their personal experience and adventurous journey with God through Jesus by His Spirit.

To those who want more out of life here on earth and desire to forget the past, to move forward into God's divine plan and purpose for their lives.

To those who will become willing and yielded vessels that will allow God use them as an extension of His mercy, grace and love to bring salvation to their generation.

To those who will love to experience God for themselves and know what it is to walk the face of this earth as children of the Most High God.

To those who want to live a life of purpose and impact, leaving behind a lasting legacy: *a long list of exploits on this short journey* here on earth.

To those seeking God diligently, who thirst and hunger after Him knowing that there are unspeakable spiritual rewards, yet to be experienced in Christ.

ACKNOWLEDGEMENTS

To *my* #HeavenlyFather,
"I have heard and read about You, as God but now I have come to know You as a loving and powerful Father."

To *the loving memory of my late* #FunDadandStepMom:
Mr. Oladipo & Mrs. Felicia Akinsanmi

To *my* #IndustriousWife, Abby; *our* #WittyDaughter, Sharon; *and* #OurLittleRoyalPrince, Elyon

To *my* #ArmorBearerMom:
Deaconess Agnes Akinsanmi

To *my* #NeverADullMoment #Siblings #OmoAkins:
Temidayo Osinuga, Lara Shogbamu, Abiola Akinsanmi, Tolu Olatoregun and Aramide Akinsanmi

To *the* #SeniorPastors *of* Jesus House, DC:
Pastors Ghandi & Omo Olaoye

To *my* #SteadfastCo-laborers:
Solomon Iyamu, Goke Dele, Oladoye Olubi, Saji Ijiyemi, Seyi Odumosu, Kunle Bello, Pastor Ade Adewole, Deacon Olubunmi Adebanjo, Olalekan Olamide, Patricia Bunting, Cheryl Lovell, Dapo Amosu, Seun Osinuga and Adeola Adegbonmire

To *the* #AssistantPastor *of* Jesus House, DC:
Pastor Olumide Ogunjuyigbe

To *the* #AssociatePastors *of* Jesus House, DC:
Pastor Chinyere Olujide
Pastor Tunde Ogungbade

To *the* #ChurchAdministrator | #ChairmanOfMinisters
Pastor Bimbo Fasosin | Pastor Ayo Fakulujo

To *my* #COI {Children of Issachar Prayer Group family}

To *the* Jesus House, DC #PrayerMinistry #Ministers
#Staff #HODs #RhampLeaders #NextGenLeaders
#Workers *and my* #Hanover1LighthouseFamily

To *my* Jesus House, DC #SpecialCrew:

Pastor Chinyere Olujide	Cheryl Lovell
Pastor Bimbo Fasosin	Bolaji Tubi
Pastor Collette Uwadia	Gladys Egbo
Deacon Michael Chidubem	Adetinuke Laoye
Deaconess Rioke Pecku	Toyin Bakare
Sister Mary Kokumo	Vivian Anugo
Mayowa Ogundiyun	Erika Barnes
Rosemary Ogbebor	Deborah Eribake
Elder Solomon Ekatah	Elder Dayo Olaiya
Femi Akinkuowo	Femi Onanuga

"We spend our early and strong years in pursuit of Success and spend our late and weak years in pursuit of Purpose."

-Toks Akinsanmi

CONTENTS

Inspiring Generations

"This book is written to help you discover who you are in Christ by sharing my spiritual journey and through this reveal how the life of Jesus here on earth is still relevant to you today."

This book is a practical guide written to inspire and encourage those who are curious about spirituality and desire to embark on their spiritual journey with God. It is for those who doubt the existence of God, who are skeptical about the idea of Christianity, or who already believe in God but want to experience more than going to church every Sunday.

God already has a plan for humanity. However, part of His plan requires us to discover how we fit in the big picture of His plan through Christ and with the help of the Holy Spirit. He wants us to know that Jesus is still relevant to our existence today. I gave my life to Christ in the year 2006, and my life has never remained the same. I discovered who I was in Christ which gave my life a new meaning and purpose. My hunger for God fueled the desire for my own experience. My spiritual journey has been much more exciting and adventurous since then, especially with the help of the Holy Spirit.

It is my desire that every Christian both young and old have an intimate relationship with God. I share my experience in this book because I know that there is more to God than what we may have heard or read. On this journey, I realize that we are the initiators of our spiritual journey.

God wants us to go beyond reading and hearing about Him but ultimately experiencing Him here on earth. Jesus came for this purpose. The bible records how Jesus lived here on earth and in it He tells us that we can do what He did, if we only believe in His name.

I pray that as you take time out of your busy schedule to read this book you will make that priceless decision to begin your journey of self-discovery, if you have not already done so. I will admonish those who have already started their journey but for some reason or the other got sidetracked to ask the Holy Spirit for help. The Holy Spirit will help you get back on the path of living a life of purpose and impact in order to leave a legacy behind for many generations.

I pray that you will earnestly seek the true meaning of your existence and I look forward to hearing about your unique experience on this spiritual journey. Your footprint in the sand of this spiritual journey leaves a trail that can be a *"landmark of hope and encouragement"* to those coming behind, who are discouraged on this narrow path to eternal life.

Kindly fasten your seatbelt, keep reading and begin to explore God's promises, knowing there is *always more* to experience in Him!

-Toks Akinsanmi

PRESENTED TO:

_____

DATE:

_____

CHAPTER 1

Priceless Treasure

"Gold is useless to those stranded in the desert but Water preserves their lives."

Isn't it ironic that the word *"Treasures"* is interpreted as a royal family's gold coins or bars, and jewelry placed in locked chests and put away in safes out of the reach of commoners? Well, I stumbled on a far greater treasure that seems to be overlooked today because it does not conform to the ideal treasure that we know. It is a book known as the *"Holy Bible."* This book says *"Again, the kingdom of heaven is like unto treasure hid in a field; the which when a man hath found, he hideth, and for joy thereof goeth and selleth all that he hath, and buyeth that field."* (Matthew 13:44)

Some years ago, I watched a movie about some men who had a treasure map to an abandoned military base where gold bars were stored in the desert. They found the gold bars but they became stranded in the desert on their way back. Eventually, they had no water to drink and were weighed down by the weight of the bags filled with gold bars so they left the gold to seek for water. Water became priceless and essential to them. It was a determining factor to their survival. The men had to make a choice to either find some water to drink and stay alive to enjoy the gold or die of thirst.

On this bright sunny memorable day *(Thursday July 7th, 2005)*, I walked into a bookstore named *"Borders"* and I bought a bible after browsing through the religious section. My very own bible! It was a big deal to me mostly because it was not my intention to go to the bookstore or to buy a bible on that day. How would I have known that walking into the bookstore and purchasing a bible on that day was the first step to discovering who I am, why I am here and what I am created to do?

I will like to take you on a journey that began when I opened the bible and began to read its glorious contents. I believe it was a life changing experience initiated by God. Prior to that very moment in the bookstore, I grew up in a Christian home and as custom, I attended Sunday school at our church which was not too far from where we lived.

At that time, I lived in Lagos, Nigeria and grew up having most of my childhood education there. Growing up, I knew there was something special and mysterious about the bible but could not put my finger on it. I observe now that the bible is a treasure that is never locked away in chests or safes though it contains priceless words of life. Bibles can be found in many homes, offices, hotels sitting on tables, in drawers and even under pillows or on shelves accumulating dust. Now we have numerous bible apps on our phones and tablets with various versions. The bible calls out for attention from every location we have it stored. The bible wants us to study, meditate and apply its principles in our daily lives. What a widely overlooked yet priceless treasure!

"Doth not wisdom cry? and understanding put forth her voice?" (Proverbs 8:1)

Many of us are familiar with the book of Psalms in the bible and we often use the psalms when we pray. Some of us may have one or two scriptures that we memorize and recite especially when faced with a challenge. However, have we truly experienced the potency and power of the treasures in the bible? The purpose of the word of God is beyond using it as a means to an end. This priceless treasure is more than just a quick fix to our problems. The word of God was written for everyone who believes to experience and live a victorious Christian life here on earth.

We have every reason to be excited about this priceless treasure made available to us all today. Jesus Christ made this treasure available to all. His treasures are not just for the rich or royal families but to nourish every soul that desires to seek after it.

"For the merchandise of it is better than the merchandise of silver, and the gain thereof than fine gold."
(Proverbs 3:14)

Today, we have the bible printed in numerous versions and languages for everyone to read and experience. Before my teenage years, I mentioned that I attended Sunday school with other kids and I was fascinated by the teachings and the stories shared from the bible. One of the books we used to read which I quickly got fascinated with was *"My Book of Bible Stories."* It had colorful pictures of bible characters and it highlighted their stories with very legible letters which were very easy and fun to read. I loved David's character especially where it had a colorful page of him playing a musical instrument in the presence of Saul. The images depict how he took down Goliath with his sling and five stones. It is interesting how Samson is usually portrayed as a hefty, guy with chiseled body features in many Christian books. However, from studying the word now, I can conclude that he was just an ordinary guy who experienced the power of God from time to time. The power of God enabled Samson to do extraordinary things. The same applies to us when we experience God's power.

As I progressed and proceeded to Junior High School, I had to take a class called Christian Religious Knowledge, which we referred to as *"CRK."* The stories in the textbooks only got more fascinating to me. However, the joy from reading the stories was quickly rubbed off by frequent take home assignments and pop up quizzes from the numerous chapters we had to cover. Also, we had to write lots of essays which made it appear more like a literature class and we had to submit them in order to pass the class.

After Junior High School, I really did not have any pressing reason to study the bible and I never had to buy one either. There were bibles around the house that each sibling claimed was theirs. I had one, a blue Gideon's New Testament pocket bible which was distributed freely to students by Christian organizations. I read it from time to time and the words inspired me, especially the Psalms and Proverbs. I memorized some scriptures which I confessed from time to time when I prayed to God. I loved to confess the scripture in *Philippians 4:13* which says *"I can do all things through Christ which strengtheneth me."* It was one of my favorite scriptures.

I found the stories told to us about David, Abraham and Jesus at Sunday school and those which I read quite fascinating. In the evenings, our Dad told us various folklore stories about the *"Tortoise and the Hare"* or *"Why the Tortoise has a bald head,"* which were amusing and entertaining. I watched folklore episodes on Television too, and I enjoyed reading and listening to the stories in the bible the same way I enjoyed those folklore stories. How was I to know that the stories in the bible had great meaning? How was I to know that great treasures lay hidden in the bible and that they were relevant to my existence and journey here on earth?

"It is the glory of God to conceal a thing: but the honour of kings is to search out a matter." (Proverbs 25:2)

"Open thou mine eyes, that I may behold wondrous things out of thy law." (Psalm 119:18)

God, in His awesomeness has concealed treasures in the bible for us to discover and those who take time to study it will ultimately enjoy the reward of their findings. If we consider the mining process involved in the search for gold, we will be amazed at the depth that miners have to dig into the earth with machineries to extract gold ore in its natural state. Sometimes, we may wonder how a book such as the bible can be a priceless treasure and of great importance to our existence. How are its contents different from any other book we have read? What we find in the bible is alive and becomes our personal revelation. The personal revelation received should have a great impact on the choices we make as we navigate our way here on earth.

Fast forward to June 1998, the month and year I came to the United States. I attended church occasionally due to my scheduled work and school routine which took most of my time. After graduating from College, I decided to start attending church faithfully. A part of me had been yearning to find a church to fellowship and hear the word of God. One of the many advices most African parents give their US bound kids is to *"Find a good church to attend."* I had made up my mind that once I graduate from College, I would find one in the area. I started to attend a church not too far from where I lived. I lived in Washington, DC at the time so I decided to attend Jesus House, DC in Silver Spring, Maryland. The church is located at the borderline of Maryland and Washington, DC.

Now we can get back to the moment after I paid for the bible. I paid for the bible that day, without knowing that my life was going to change forever in the next few months. I had acquired a book that contained priceless treasures of life. These treasures are different from the world's idea of treasures. The promises found in the bible are alive and real.

"And I will give thee the treasures of darkness, and hidden riches of secret places, that thou mayest know that I, the Lord, which call thee by thy name, am the God of Israel." (Isaiah 45:3)

My journey began that very moment I walked into the bookstore. Did I know that a book can completely change my life? I was not aware that purchasing that bible on that day marked the beginning of God's call on my life through Jesus Christ. God wanted to show me those things that belonged to me in His word. I began to read the bible and as I read it, I got more curious about the things that I read. How exciting to discover what lies within each page. I finally *"owned"* a Bible. I had bibles given to me prior to that time but this was different I could not still explain why I stopped by Borders Bookstore to purchase a Bible!

This moment reminded me of a movie I watched when I was much younger titled *"The NeverEnding Story."* The movie was about a boy named Bastian. On his way to school, he runs into a bookstore to hide from some bullies. He stumbled on a book titled *"The NeverEnding Story"* while he was in the bookstore. Bastian took the book and begins to read it in the school attic. He discovers that it was about *"Fantasia,"* a fantasy land threatened by *"The Nothing,"* a darkness that destroys everything it touches. For the kingdom to survive, it needed the help of a human child. The book got more interesting to Bastian as he read it. As he continued reading, he began to identify with the character in the book. He realizes that the storyline of the book describes him and at the end, he begins to wonder if Fantasia is real and needs him to save it.

This story is similar to our true adventure as Christians when we experience the word of God in our lives. However, the difference is that the bible is not a book filled with fantasies but is alive and real for everyone to experience for themselves. The word of God actually makes our Christian walk exciting and fun. We realize that the treasures in the word of God make our walk adventurous and not religious from routines and activities which become boring. The word of God is full of exploits that we can learn about and do as we strive to build our relationship with Jesus.

"Wherefore do ye spend money for that which is not bread? and your labour for that which satisfieth not? hearken diligently unto me, and eat ye that which is good, and let your soul delight itself in fatness." (Isaiah 55:2)

It is amazing to know that we spend a great portion of our finances on things that are temporary, yet our source of life is not material but spiritual. Our body received life from a gentle breath from God. How wonderful to find out that we can experience the written word of God. We are able to do exploits like the disciples of Jesus did, if we only believe. I continued to take time out every day to read my bible. At that time, I worked as an external auditor with PricewaterhouseCoopers which involved frequent travel. As I read the bible, I stumbled on a great treasure that had to become a reality which was to get baptized by immersion. I soon discovered that I would need more time to study my bible and be practical with what I read. There was a greater desire to experience the treasures deeply embedded in the word of God. His word brought life and fresh breath to my spirit, soul and body. I was like a kid in a candy store. Ah! All these candy waiting to meet with my taste buds. Oh, so many treasures we have hidden in Christ. As I read further, I understood why Jesus said in John 4:32, "... *I have meat to eat that ye know not of.*" Jesus was letting his disciples know that His words are nourishing and brings life. The words in the bible contain great treasures yet to be discovered and experienced.

"It is the spirit that quickeneth; the flesh profiteth nothing: the words that I speak unto you, they are spirit, and they are life." *(John 6:63)*

As I read about Christ, I discovered that He gave us a pattern to follow to begin our spiritual journey and attain spiritual maturity *(which I will go further into from Chapter 3)*. I got curious and determined not to cut corners but to apply the principles received from the written word in my life. I stumbled upon this pattern in the book of Exodus when God called Moses. God told him to build a tabernacle where the Israelites would go to worship Him. God revealed the blueprint for building the tabernacle and how the Israelites should approach Him in worship.

"And look that thou make them after their pattern, which was shewed thee in the mount." (Exodus 25:40)

Prior to the birth of Moses, the Israelites enjoyed freedom and favor in Egypt in the days of Joseph. However, after Joseph died, a new King who did not know Joseph took over Egypt and the people of Israel were made slaves. They lived in bondage for over four hundred years and cried out to God for help because of their affliction.

Fortunately for them, Moses was sent as an answer to their prayers for deliverance. Moses was to lead them to Canaan *(the Promised Land)* where they could experience those treasures which God promised them by the covenant He made with Abraham. God desired to reveal to them His best kept secrets hidden in His words. They were meant to experience the freedom these treasures would bring for themselves. God was trying to introduce a new way of life to them through the pattern He gave to Moses. However, the treasures of God were yet to be revealed to them. Over the years, bondage had robbed them of the liberty they could have enjoyed from the word of God. They were yet to know God as Yaweh (*meaning "I am"*).

The good news is that God desires a personal exodus for everyone. This exodus is not necessarily physical but definitely spiritual. However, you have to make a personal decision to take that step of faith and press in deeper on this journey with God. His treasures are priceless and fulfilling. The word of God brings ultimate satisfaction to the very core of your being if you only let it into your world. Colossians 1:25-27 lets us know that the mystery behind who we are will be revealed to us as we continue on the path of discovering the "I" in ChrIst.

"25 Whereof I am made a minister, according to the dispensation of God which is given to me for you, to fulfil the word of God; 26 Even the mystery which hath been hid from ages and from generations, but now is made manifest to his saints: 27 To whom God would make known what is the riches of the glory of this mystery among the Gentiles; which is Christ in you, the hope of glory."

There is more to life than what we physically see. God wants to introduce us to His true identity. God is a Spirit and those that desire to experience Him can only do that in the spirit. God referred to Himself as *"Yaweh"* to Moses and He wanted the same with the Israelites. God wants the same experience for you too. He is the same yesterday today and forever.

God gave Moses a blueprint for building the tabernacle where the Israelites would worship Him. From the pattern God gave Moses *(which will be discussed as you read further)*, we will be able to determine where we are spiritually with God. It is a spiritual map that lets us know if we are still outside the tabernacle, in the outer court, in the Holy Place or abiding in the Holy of Holies. On this journey, God wants to take us from the outer court to the inner court to abide and fellowship with Him. This journey can be accomplished today through Jesus Christ.

"Jesus saith unto him, I am the way, the truth, and the life: no man cometh unto the Father, but by me." (John 14:6)

God sent His Son, Jesus to die on the cross because by His crucifixion and resurrection a divine relationship with man can now be established by His Spirit. The inner court is where the relationship is established. Jesus is the way to the inner chambers of God. You can make that priceless decision to begin your journey today!

CHAPTER 2

In the beginning

---

*"Seeing ourselves in the image of God
requires a relationship sustained by
deliberately being in His presence."*

I n order to properly diagnose a problem, we have to go back to the where the problem started. In the beginning, God created us in His own image. He had a plan for us to be like Him. God the Father, the Son and the Holy Spirit had an agreement to create us in His very image so that we can dominate and rule the earth.

Our identity was settled long before creation in the heavenly boardroom when it was said *"let us make man in our image" (Genesis 1:26)*. God let Jeremiah know that He knew him before he was formed in his mother's womb and had a plan for him *(Jeremiah 29:11)*. However, our identity was stolen from us in the Garden of Eden. God created Adam and Eve in His image and their identity was established by His divine relationship with them. He came to them in the cool of the day to reveal more of Himself to them. His presence sustained them. The revelation of our image in God requires a relationship which is sustained by being in His presence.

From the scriptures, we observe that after God created Adam and Eve, He placed them in a garden where they had access to His presence. This detail was deliberate and important for us to fully understand our divine image and identity in God. We have His Divine Nature and Attributes *(which I refer to as "DNA")* that is to be revealed by His Spirit. The devil knows that our image is sustained by the presence of God. His plan is to tarnish our image or how we see ourselves by destroying our relationship with God which started in Genesis 3:1-5:

> *The revelation of our image in God requires a relationship sustained by being in His presence.*

"1 Now the serpent was more subtil than any beast of the field which the Lord God had made. And he said unto the woman, Yea, hath God said, Ye shall not eat of every tree of the garden? 2 And the woman said unto the serpent, We may eat of the fruit of the trees of the garden: 3 But of the

fruit of the tree which is in the midst of the garden, God hath said, Ye shall not eat of it, neither shall ye touch it, lest ye die. 4 And the serpent said unto the woman, Ye shall not surely die: 5 For God doth know that in the day ye eat thereof, then your eyes shall be opened, and ye shall be as gods, knowing good and evil."

The devil once enjoyed the presence of God so his goal is to destroy our relationship with God by lying to us about our identity everyday even as he did in the beginning. The scripture mentioned that the serpent was more *"Subtil"* *(which means deceitful, crafty, cunning, treacherous, deceptive)* than any other creature created. For this reason, the devil used the serpent as a vessel to speak to Eve. The serpent questioned if God had asked Eve not to eat of the fruit of the tree in the garden. The purpose of that question was to challenge the authority of God's word given to them and cause doubt. Our identity is being challenged every day by the kingdom of darkness. The devil wanted to find out if they were going to obey God's words. The devil tests our obedience to God's words.

Today, the devil has devised ways to tell us that *"our eyes will be opened"* to test us just like he did with Adam and Eve. However, his ways only lead us in rebellion

31

against God. The devil says to us today that we can become our own god. He makes us believe that we do not need God or have to regard His word. The devil likes to make us feel like we are wise enough to decipher good from evil on our own. God came back in the cool of the day to fellowship with them and they realized they were naked. They had been robbed of their divine identity in broad daylight! Like Adam and Eve, we have become self-conscious and ashamed of how God created us. For instance, in our society today, it is a shame to say you are opposed to pre-marital sex or to say that you are a virgin.

"11 And he said, Who told thee that thou wast naked? Hast thou eaten of the tree, whereof I commanded thee that thou shouldest not eat? 12 And the man said, The woman whom thou gavest to be with me, she gave me of the tree, and I did eat." (Genesis 3:11-12)

From this scripture, we note that eating the fruit from the tree changed their divine identity. Like Adam and Eve, we may have been through a negative situation and the outcome has shaped our identity. We observe that it is the simplest decision that gradually alters our divine identity. Also, it is the simplest decision of accepting Christ that can restore us to our original and divine identity.

Our identity can be received from different sources outside of God which becomes our belief system. Our belief system is made up of information received from our culture and the people or situations that directly or indirectly influence our lives over time. God asked Adam who told him that he was naked. The devil knew that they will become naked if they ate the fruit. This was his deception. They were already covered by God's presence. God knew something had gone wrong when He saw them and they hid from Him. They became self-conscious and ashamed of their God given identity. They began to alter their identity by covering themselves with leaves.

Our true identity was tampered with in the Garden of Eden and we see its effect in humanity today. Due to pride, the devil was banished from God's presence along with a third of the heavenly angels who decided to go him. His original name is Lucifer and he was in charge of worship in heaven. The devil knows a lot about God's presence and the power of our true identity in Christ. Our fallen nature is the cause of our identity crisis. We can conclude that our fallen nature and identity crisis came about when Adam and Eve fell for the devil's deception in the Garden of Eden.

Our False Identity

> *"Our false identity stems from an inner desire and longing for acceptance from external sources."*

"What belongs to you, but others use it more than you do?" The answer is *"your name."* Your name is what people call you more than you do. We are the sum total of our experiences with others and our environment from birth up till now. Our identity has been built on things that are temporary which will eventually expire.

"24 Therefore whosoever heareth these sayings of mine, and doeth them, I will liken him unto a wise man, which built his house upon a rock: 25 And the rain descended, and the floods came, and the winds blew, and beat upon that house; and it fell not: for it was founded upon a rock. 26 And every one that heareth these sayings of mine, and doeth them not, shall be likened unto a foolish man, which built his house upon the sand: 27 And the rain descended, and the floods came, and the winds blew, and beat upon that house; and it fell: and great was the fall of it." (Matthew 7: 24-27)

Our identity has to be built on solid ground not on sand. *"Sand"* here means a false identity that cannot sustain our true nature. It is necessary for us to build our identity on Jesus, our rock. Our true identity can only be found in Him. The way we will stand the pressures of life will depend on the strength of the foundation that our identity is built on. Our identity can be solid as a rock if only it is found in Jesus.

Our identity can be formed and shaped by what we read or view on media platforms *(i.e. Television, Magazines and Social Media)* and learn from friends, family members, and school. We begin to alter our identity and how God has created us to fit in. Without Christ we are empty and we fill that void with anything that can only give us temporary satisfaction. God has created us with a void that He only can fill for us to be truly satisfied.

Our false identity stems from an inner desire and longing for acceptance from external sources. We derive our identity from how much money we have in the bank, our physical appearance, our family name or heritage, our nick name, our title or status in society, our nationality, our race, the fraternity we belong to, our marital status, our political party, our skill or profession, the church we attend, the school we attend or attended, our favorite sport team, the number of *"likes"* on social media or even where we live. These are not our true identity in Christ. Our identity was tampered with from the time of Adam and Eve, when Eve was tempted in the Garden of Eden. Adam blamed Eve and Eve blamed the serpent for this identity crisis. However, God's remedy for restoring our identity back to the way it was before the temptation in the Garden of Eden is through His Son, Jesus.

In the society we live in today, we blame someone else for the identity received outside of God. After examining ourselves, we will find that the source of our identity is from our culture and our environment. We have exposed ourselves to these two factors over time and they have directly or indirectly influenced our lives at a particular time or over a period of time. There is a cumulative effect on our true identity which affects how we see ourselves and view life. In the Garden of Eden, the serpent represents anything that is not of God or in His word. God gave them His word but the devil came along to deceive them. We operate below our potential when we do not know who and whose we are. False identity can also be received through other deceptive mediums that we may have exposed ourselves to such as reading horoscopes, psychic reading via palm reading and tarot card reading. These sources are not from God and should be avoided.

All of these devices are crafted by the devil to keep us outside of God's plan. This issue of identity crisis did not begin with you. It began in the Garden of Eden with Adam and Eve when they fell for the serpent's craftiness. The deception was by a crafty being called *"Satan"* who stripped them of their original identity. The good news is that God has a divine plan to restore and redeem our true identity through His Son, Jesus Christ!

One of the first questions Moses asked God was *"Who will I say sent me?"* God said *"I am that I am."* God's identity has been established with Himself. We have to do the same. However, we cannot do it without God. God resolved the issue of identity crisis with Moses by the personal encounter he had at the burning bush. God told him to throw his Staff on the ground and it turned into a snake. God asked him to pick it up again and it turned back into his staff. God asked Moses to put his hand in his cloak and his hands became leprous. God told him to put it back and his hand was restored. God gave Moses a personal encounter so that he can know and identify with Him as Yaweh.

A man named Paul was persecuting the early Christians for talking about Jesus. However, on his way to Damascus, Jesus appeared to him and revealed Himself to him. He stopped persecuting the church and became one of the most powerful Christians in his time. The first thing God does is to reveal Himself to us through His word and by His Spirit before using us. We are transformed by His word and Spirit to remove any trace of doubt caused by our false identity.

Jesus knew who He was and desires the same for every believer in His kingdom. Jesus asked His disciples:

"...But whom say ye that I am? And Peter answereth and saith unto him, Thou art the Christ." (Mark 8:29).

You should be unwavering about who you are as followers of Christ. You are the child of the Most High God! Like Moses and Paul, you need a personal encounter with God which is possible to you too. As we continue to read further, we will discover that our true identity is rooted and grounded in our knowledge of the Almighty God.

CHAPTER 3

The Journey begins

*"Your journey toward eternal life begins
with your decision to follow Jesus today."*

Our Spiritual journey begins with the pattern that God gave Moses as mentioned in Chapter 1. It is the blueprint for our pilgrimage here on earth. We can use it to track where we are spiritually with God. Our spiritual age begins to tick not when we are born into this world but from the day we surrender our lives to Christ. The Israelites began their spiritual pilgrimage the day Moses led them out of Egypt from bondage. As mentioned earlier, my journey started when I walked into the bookstore, bought a bible and started reading it. Our mind is the first place transformation begins as we feed it with new information from God's word.

"And be not conformed to this world: but be ye transformed by the renewing of your mind, that ye may prove what is

that good, and acceptable, and perfect, will of God."
(Romans 12:2)

As we recall, Moses had a challenge after he led the Israelites out of Egypt. Moses had encountered God who set him free from his past. His mind became renewed and transformed but the people he was trying to lead into freedom were still slaves in their minds and ways. They could not understand what Moses had experienced with God at the burning bush neither had they experienced Him for themselves.

As Moses led them out of Egypt, whenever they faced any challenge or obstacle, their first response was the desire to go back to Egypt where they were once slaves. Slavery was their identity and comfort zone. It was all they knew so we can begin to understand the frustrations Moses had with them. However, it was not their fault as their minds were not renewed and they had not known Yaweh for themselves. God's plan was to deliver them from bondage so that they could worship Him and have their own encounter with Him.

"And the Lord spake unto Moses, Go unto Pharaoh, and say unto him, Thus saith the Lord, Let my people go, that they

may serve me." (Exodus 8:1)

How could they worship and serve a God that they had not encountered? God called Moses and showed him the way to worship Him. Moses was tasked to lead the Israelites from bondage and show them how to follow the same pattern of worship revealed to him so that they too could experience God for themselves. Moses went ahead to build the tabernacle according to the pattern revealed to him by God as documented in book of Exodus from Chapter 25 to Chapter 31.

Confession and Repentance

"Repentance has to do with confessing and turning away from our sinful ways."

As I studied the word my mind became renewed. I wanted more! Why? I had asked God for forgiveness for my sinful lifestyle. Repentance has to do with confessing and completely turning away from sin.

"I came not to call the righteous, but sinners to repentance."
(Luke 5:32)

"As a dog returneth to his vomit, so a fool returneth to his folly." (Proverbs 26:11)

Jesus Christ came to redeem anyone that will forsake their old ways and turn to Him for salvation. From studying the pattern given to Moses in the book of Exodus, the first structure the Israelites met once they came in through the gate of the tabernacle was the *"Altar of Burnt Offering."* The altar was the place for burning animal sacrifices. Once an Israelite laid hands on the animal to be sacrificed his or her sin and guilt was transferred to the animal. The Priest slaughters the animal, sprinkles its blood in front of the Veil of the Holy Place, burns the sacrifice, and pours the rest of it at the bottom of the altar for their sins to be covered each year.

Today, we follow the same pattern given to Moses but through Jesus Christ. All we have to do is to ask God for forgiveness in a prayer commonly referred to as *"The Sinner's Prayer."* This prayer is done from the heart when we speak to God in repentance and acknowledge that we have sinned, confess our sins, decide to turn away from those sins and accept Jesus as our personal Lord and Savior. You can take a few minutes to ask God for forgiveness right now, if you have not already done so.

Once you have done this, believe that you have been forgiven *(1 John 1:9)*.

Baptized by Immersion

> *"We are submerged in water to immerge as a new creature born into a new life in Christ like a butterfly out of its cocoon."*

Reading the word was so exciting! I continued to read further and at the same time asking God what was next after repentance. From digging deeper into my newly found bible treasure, I made the priceless decision to continue this journey by getting baptized by immersion. I read where Jesus was talking to Nicodemus in John 3:5-6:

"5 Jesus answered, Verily, verily, I say unto thee, Except a man be born of water and of the Spirit, he cannot enter into the kingdom of God. 6 That which is born of the flesh is flesh; and that which is born of the Spirit is spirit."

What does it mean to be born of water? From the pattern given to Moses, the *"Brazen Laver"* or *"Basin"* was the next piece after the Altar of Burnt offering. It was filled with water for the Priests to wash their hands and their feet before entering the Holy Place. To be born of water is about the re-birth, a new life in Christ like a butterfly coming out of its cocoon. It is the prerequisite for entering into the kingdom of God. How exciting! I wanted to experience all of that for myself.

"3 *Know ye not, that so many of us as were baptized into Jesus Christ were baptized into his death? 4 Therefore we are buried with him by baptism into death: that like as Christ was raised up from the dead by the glory of the Father, even so we also should walk in newness of life.*" (Romans 6:3-4)

> The word of God usually requires us to do simple things that will eventually produce great results.

How glorious it is to walk in this newness of life! I longed to experience this for myself. I desired it. I wondered about how God's plans for us are so simple yet powerful. We can understand why the people in the bible reacted to the words of the prophets the way they did. It sounded too simple to comprehend. The word of God usually requires us to do simple things that will eventually produce great results. The ways of God may appear foolish to us yet they bring eternal value.

"But God hath chosen the foolish things of the world to confound the wise; and God hath chosen the weak things of the world to confound the things which are mighty." (1 Corinthians 1:27)

There is an account of a man named Naaman, a great soldier in his days. He had a contagious disease called *"Leprosy."* Elisha, the prophet asked him to go dip himself in the Jordan River seven times in order to be healed. At first, he refused to do it because it seemed too simple. However, after being persuaded by one of his servants, he dipped himself in the river and was completely healed. This is similar to the simplicity of water baptism that we are required to do today.

"Then went he down, and dipped himself seven times in Jordan, according to the saying of the man of God: and his flesh came again like unto the flesh of a little child, and he was clean." (2 Kings 5: 14)

As I kept on reading, weeks turned to months and by the end of the year 2005, I decided to partake in the 2006 January Corporate fast. I had read and realized the significance of fasting in the life of a Christian. Growing up, I had an idea about what it meant to fast. As children and young adults, we did not fully understand why we should give up food for any reason. The topic of fasting is not strange to those who grew up in Africa. We tend to fast either by choice or skip meals to stay within our budget.

In Nigeria, fasting is practiced by Muslims and Christians. Many Christians had family members who were Muslims. Some Christians even joined their Muslim family members to observe the Ramadan fast. Once a fast is declared, we were all required not to eat or drink from midnight to 6pm each day for the number of days of the fast. However, there isn't much emphasis on fasting in the western world. Fasting is a free will exercise and is done in a variety of ways and options. Fasting, as practiced in the bible is abstaining from food and entertainment to seek God. Some kings were known to have discontinued food and entertainment in the palace when they fasted to seek God, the King of Kings. It is important to note that fasting is for a purpose. Our fasting period should include praying and studying the bible to be spiritually effective.

In January 2006, I commenced the corporate fast declared by the church for the whole month and I made a decision to complete it. My major reason was that I wanted more of God and was actually excited to go on the fast. I had a great desire and hunger for more of God. This decision brought an excitement within me. I believed that something great will come out of it though I did not know what would happen along the way. This made it even much more adventurous! I had read Isaiah 58 and was excited about the blessings that come with prayer and fasting.

I had fasted in the past but I had never gone on a thirty day fast before. However, I looked forward to each day expecting new experiences in God. I believe this fasting exercise was a personal breakthrough for me. It marked the beginning of the sanctification process that every believer goes through on this spiritual journey. I was excited about this re-birth experience and looked forward to embracing the new way of life in Christ.

"Howbeit this kind goeth not out but by prayer and fasting." *(Matthew 17:21)*

This scripture further buttressed my belief that it is essential to fast in preparation for any spiritual activity or event we desire to partake in. I lost the desire for my old ways. It gave me strength to do the things God wanted me to do. I felt renewed and energized after the fast. I loved to dance to dancehall reggae music and I had lots of the tapes and CD collections at that time. However, after the fast, I broke and trashed them all. I lost the desire for them and continued to study the word of God daily. Also, I used to go clubbing with my friends but I realized I had lost the desire for the club scene. After the fast, an event was organized at the club and a famous dancehall reggae artiste from Jamaica was in town to perform. My friends called me with so much enthusiasm for us to attend because we loved his music but I declined. They were puzzled. It was a new life for me now especially with the word of God becoming even more real in my life. I had found a new love.

During the fast, I took a few minutes to pray during my lunch time at work. I sat with my co-workers after prayers in the cafeteria and had conversations with them while they ate. I explained to them that I was on a fast for an extended period when they asked and they respected my decision. I had conversations with my heavenly Father throughout the day. I took walks to pray during my short breaks. It was a new adventure and an exciting relationship with my heavenly Father!

As I kept on reading my bible, I realized that the next thing I had to do was to get baptized as I mentioned earlier. One of the main reasons I decided to do it was that Jesus Christ who we follow was baptized too. Also, I observed from studying my bible that it was customary for Peter, Paul and the other disciples to have those who accepted Jesus as their Lord and Savior baptized immediately after their confession and repentance.

"Then they that gladly received his word were baptized: and the same day there were added unto them about three thousand souls." (Acts 2:41)

How glorious it is to have three thousand people baptized by immersion in one day! Also, another reason for getting baptized was that I wanted to experience that new life in Christ as described in Romans 6 and John 3:1-15.

With my current job, I had travel obligations which I enjoyed since I love to travel. However, in order to attend the baptismal class and other church obligations, I made the decision to give up the perks that came with the job position so that I can have more time to do the things of God. I mentioned my preference for a job position with a more stable work schedule to God in prayers after which I posted my resume online. We know that when we pray according to His will, God is faithful to grant our petitions.

Some weeks later, I got a call from a recruiter at IBM. I did a phone interview and was in the process of scheduling an appointment to meet with a partner from IBM when my current job scheduled me for a five week assignment out of town. I spoke to the IBM recruiter notifying him that I would be out of town for five weeks and I left for the assignment. I returned from the assignment and got a call from the recruiter at IBM the next day after I returned that the offer was still open to me for a second interview. He informed me that he placed my name in his calendar for a second interview on my return from my assignment. Mind blowing! God is as so amazing to keep the job for me for over a month. I was certain that the job was for me.

I attended the interview and the preferences I asked for in prayer were acknowledged at the interview. Also, the desired location and the distance of the office location to my home were what I asked for in prayer. It is refreshing to know that my desires mentioned in conversations with my heavenly Father are heard and answered. God had answered my prayers in times past but I felt more of His leading and presence throughout the situation.

I went ahead and signed up for the 5-Week Baptismal Class. Each day, I looked forward to taking the class and finally get baptized. Although, I had studied about why we should be baptized and what happens afterwards, I looked forward to my experience.

On Sunday March 5th, 2006, I received a phone call from Nigeria that my father passed on. Oh! What a great loss! I realized what 1 Corinthians 15:55 says *"O death, where is thy sting? O grave, where is thy victory?"* However, in all of this I knew that God had given me victory over the sting of my father's death. I know that God loves me so much and has a plan for me. God went ahead to bring me into His kingdom to show me a greater love before my father passed on. God's plan was to save me from destruction because He knows what He has planned ahead for me. I believe God knew the love I had for my father and He saved me just in time before His death.

"For I know the thoughts that I think toward you, saith the Lord, thoughts of peace, and not of evil, to give you an expected end." (Jeremiah 29:11)

The words in the bible I had read over the past few months began to soothe and comfort me during my loss, especially when no one was there. I knew God as a comforter and His words were alive and real to me. God continued to strengthen me as I drew strength from His word daily. One scripture that stood out to me through it all was Isaiah 48:10-11:

"10 Behold, I have refined thee, but not with silver; I have chosen thee in the furnace of affliction. 11 For mine own sake, even for mine own sake, will I do it: for how should my name be polluted? and I will not give my glory unto another."

I prepared for my baptismal class and finally I got baptized by immersion on Wednesday April 5th, 2006. It was a refreshing experience. I was fully immersed in water and I embraced the new life. I was excited knowing its significance. The old has passed away and I am a new creature. I am alive in Christ! Baptism is a Greek word, *"Baptizo"* which means to be fully immersed and cleansed. I knew the significance of baptism was spiritual and that I was on the right path because I got baptized like Jesus and His disciples did. I treasured this unforgettable moment of my spiritual journey and cherished every memory of it.

Nothing happened physically immediately after the water baptism but I knew something spiritually significant happened to me after emerging from the water. I have a new life in Christ! I am a new creature on the path to discover who God has created me to be. I went home expectant and ready for the next experience.

As a new creature in Christ, this propelled my desire and thirst as I yearned to know more about the deep things of God. I realized that the scriptures revealed more about the presence of God to me and I acknowledged His presence in my life after being baptized by immersion. I had a greater desire to study the word of God and spent much more time in prayer. I realized that there is still more that God has in store for me to experience. We cannot place God in a box. There is no limit to what we can experience in God.

Moses was sent to deliver the Israelites from Egypt with God's divine plan for them to worship Him. Moses brought them out with God's mighty power at work in his life. Our spiritual awakening begins when we have a personal encounter with God. We begin as we make our journey away from the kingdom of darkness into God's marvelous light.

"Who hath delivered us from the power of darkness, and hath translated us into the kingdom of his dear Son." (Colossians 1:13)

All we have done from when we were born up till now without Jesus are outside the plan of God for our lives. God wants us to break away from those things that have held us bound as slaves subjecting us to the elements of this world. We are designed by God to rule and have dominion not over our fellow human beings but over the elements of the heavens and earth. God, through Moses parted the red sea and brought them out on dry ground into the wilderness so they can experience more of Him. God told Moses to build a tabernacle as a pattern of worship which we have read so far is relevant to us today in our walk with Him. Exodus 25:8 says *"And let them make me a sanctuary; that I may dwell among them."*

Our spiritual journey is very similar to the exodus of the Israelites from Egypt. Exodus means to *"Depart"* or *"Exit"* and in this context to depart or exit from bondage. They were slaves for over four hundred years and their deliverance came through Moses. Today, we need an exodus from bodily sickness and spiritual, financial, emotional, geographic bondages. Our exodus will involve how we deal with hurts, failures, disappointments and regrets caused by these types of burden or bondages.

From studying the pattern of the tabernacle given to Moses by God, we observe the same principles of deliverance today through Christ. Jesus came to bring an exodus to us just like Moses did for the Israelites. Jesus came to die for us on the cross taking our sins upon Himself so that we may move from our past into this new and abundant life. Freedom was personified by Christ when He left the comfort of heaven to be crucified on the cross for our sakes. Jesus started His journey by being baptized by John, the Baptist in Jordan River.

"13 Then cometh Jesus from Galilee to Jordan unto John, to be baptized of him. 14 But John forbad him, saying, I have need to be baptized of thee, and comest thou to me? 15 And Jesus answering said unto him, Suffer it to be so now: for thus it becometh us to fulfil all righteousness. Then he suffered him. 16 And Jesus, when he was baptized, went up straightway out of the water: and, lo, the heavens were opened unto him, and he saw the Spirit of God descending like a dove, and lighting upon him: 17 And lo a voice from heaven, saying, This is my beloved Son, in whom I am well pleased." (Matthew 3:13-17)

Isn't it amazing that Jesus Christ humbled himself to get baptized? He did not have to do it but in the scripture above, He told John that it was the right thing for Him to do. Jesus came to fulfil what was written about Him. It is amazing to note that the heavens are opened to us after we get baptized by immersion as stated in verse 16, *"...and, lo, the heavens were opened unto him, and he saw the Spirit of God descending like a dove, and lighting upon him."* We have access to a whole new world if we continue to press in to experience more of God. The spiritual world is real and open to us to explore with the help of the Holy Spirit. Jesus saw the Holy Spirit descend upon Him immediately after He got baptized by immersion.

Reading further, we will note that Jesus Christ got baptized by immersion and He experienced the baptism of the Holy Spirit too! He was on His journey to fulfil all that was written about Him which included water baptism. You can be on the path of doing those things Jesus Christ did, if you make that decision today to get baptized. Don't put it off to later. I did it and my life has never remained the same. Like the butterfly out of its cocoon, you are promised a new life ahead with great adventures in Christ.

CHAPTER 4

Holy Spirit Baptism

"The great and lasting works that Jesus
did can be accomplished through us by
the supernatural help of the Holy Spirit."

The topic or idea of the Holy Spirit or Holy Ghost has been one of much controversy outside the church and interestingly within the church. Those outside the church consider it *"Spooky"* or *"Weird"* and those within the church believe that it was only given to the *"early church"* and not to be used today.

Most religions desire to know God, the Father. They agree that there is a creator of heaven and earth and desire to relate with Him. Other religions profess that Jesus, the Son was a *"Prophet"* or a *"Messenger"* while the idea of the Holy Spirit is a phenomena that we cannot wrap our minds around. Today, the Holy Spirit is quickly rejected or ignored by many.

Is it the name *"Holy Spirit"* or *"Holy Ghost"* that makes this very important person not openly or freely discussed even amongst Christians? Many avoid talking about Him altogether and those that speak about Him have a limited knowledge of who He is. We do not know what we are missing without a relationship with the Holy Spirit.

First of all, the Holy Spirit is a person. Having our mind renewed about His personality will help our relationship with Him. The greater works mentioned by Jesus before ascending to heaven cannot be done without the Holy Spirit. We have to embrace the idea of

> *The greater works mentioned by Jesus before ascending to heaven cannot be done without the Holy Spirit.*

the person of the Holy Spirit before we can do those things Christ promised that we will do when He left the earth. He promised to send us another comforter and helper in order to finish well and strong.

Luke 24:49 *"And, behold, I send the promise of my Father upon you: but tarry ye in the city of Jerusalem, until ye be endued with power from on high."*

Once again, it is important to note the response Jesus gave Nicodemus about the two baptisms which are being born of water and of the Spirit and its relation to entering the kingdom of God:

"Jesus answered, Verily, verily, I say unto thee, Except a man be born of water and of the Spirit, he cannot enter into the kingdom of God. 6 That which is born of the flesh is flesh; and that which is born of the Spirit is spirit." *(John 3:5-6)*

Jesus emphasized that without these two baptisms taking place in our lives we cannot enter and experience the kingdom of God. These two experiences are God's prerequisite for entering and experiencing the spiritual realm to discover who we truly are in the kingdom of God.

An Empowered Me!

"An account of my personal encounter with the Holy Spirit."

I will share how I got baptized and began to experience God's presence in my life. Here is an article I wrote and shared with my family and friends with details describing my memorable encounter with the Holy Spirit.

The best moment of my life was when I gave my life to Christ and encountered the Holy Spirit. Kindly take a moment to read the details because it can happen to you too and those who already experienced this can relate to it. Who is the Holy Spirit?

"And I will pray the Father, and he shall give you another Comforter, that he may abide with you for ever."
(John 14:16)

The Holy Spirit is *"another Comforter"*, a second comforter succeeding the first who is Jesus, and both were given by the Father. Do you say, *"I do not understand this?"* Who can understand this? God would not have us use head knowledge but receive the Holy Spirit in our hearts in order to experience Him. There are three persons-in-one Godhead revealed as God, the Father; God, the Son (Jesus Christ) and God, the Holy Spirit. We are also a mysterious trinity of spirit, soul and body. The *'how"* is a mystery. It is a matter of having faith and of personal encounter that produces revelation.

"The Holy Spirit will guide you into all truth: for he shall not speak of himself; but whatsoever he shall hear, that shall he speak: and he will show you things to come." (John 16:13)

In the ordinary affairs of life, we focus on the facts and believe them without worrying about the *"how"* of things. Who can explain how food sustains life, how light illuminates objects or how sound is received as waves and perceived by the brain? It is the fact we know and believe, but the *"how"* we refer to as a mystery unrevealed. We cannot understand how Jesus turned water into wine, how He multiplied five loaves of bread and two fish to feed five thousand people, how He stilled the stormy sea, how He opened blind eyes, healed lepers and raised the dead by a word. However, we believe the facts. Wireless telegraphic messages are sent over vast wastes of ocean via telephones, fax, and internet. We believe it and we do not worry ourselves about how it works.

After giving my life to Christ, I got baptized by immersion on April 5th, 2006 which was a renewing experience. As a new creature in Christ, I wanted more. The scriptures revealed to me the fact about the personality of the Holy Spirit and I acknowledged His presence in my life after being baptized. I started to ponder on what the apostles and disciples spoke about the Holy Ghost on and after the day of Pentecost. Immediately after being filled with the Holy Spirit, Peter stood before the people, and said:

This is that which was spoken by the prophet Joel, "And it shall come to pass in the last days, saith God, I will pour out of My Spirit upon all flesh." (Acts 2:16-17).

Also, in 1 Corinthians 2:12-13, Paul says *"Now we have received, not the spirit of the world, but the Spirit which is of God; that we might know the things that are freely given to us of God. Which things also we speak, not in the words which man's wisdom teacheth, but which the Holy Ghost teacheth."*

I pondered, *"So if we know these words, why can't we also know the Teacher of these words?"* I shall never forget my joy, mixed with great excitement and expectation received from the revelation of these words. I continued attending church, searching the scriptures daily, checking my heart, humbling my soul with fasting, and praying fervently to God for a pure heart and for the baptism with the Holy Ghost to speak in tongues. On one Sunday, an announcement was made in my local church

(Jesus House, DC) about the *"Holy Spirit Day"* event which was the grand finale of the 10-Week Foundation Class ending in the month of August. I noted the date and planned to attend. As the class proceeded, we were taught about the person of the Holy Spirit, the gifts and fruit of the Holy Spirit. We started our prayers by welcoming the presence of the Holy Spirit. The ministers laid hands on me and encouraged me to keep praying until I received the gift. As I prayed, I asked God to purify my heart. I forgave those who offended me and asked God for forgiveness. I prayed for the gift of speaking in tongues and lo and behold, as we kept on praying, I felt warm inside and I started praying in another language. I continued praying in tongues, saying to myself, *"This is pretty cool!"*

Contrary to what people think I didn't feel controlled by any force. All I felt was an overwhelming feeling of love mixed with inner peace and unspeakable joy as tears filled my eyes. My heart melted like wax and Jesus Christ was revealed to my spiritual consciousness. At that moment I knew that God, the Holy Spirit was in this love, and that this love was God, for *"God is love."* I have tasted of God and His goodness. Psalm 34:8 says *"O taste and see that the Lord is good..."*

Growing up, I read the bible as a novel, spiritually blind to its content and just intrigued by the stories. I realized that there is a great difference between quoting our favorite scriptures like *"The Lord's Prayer,"* John 3:16 or Psalm 23 and experiencing them. This encounter brings an assurance to my heart that what I read in the bible is real because I experienced it myself like the apostles did on the day of Pentecost *(as revealed in Acts 2:1-6).* Now I know that the blessings and promises of the bible can occur in my life, if only I believe. I haven't stopped praying in tongues since then.

From that day, I realized I had received my private prayer language. It is an assurance that the Holy Spirit abides in me. I realized that God gave me a heavenly language to help me communicate better with Him. This is the best gift ever because He *(the Holy Spirit)* prays to God on my behalf and witnesses to my spirit that I am a child of God. Also, knowing that the Holy Spirit comes with spiritual gifts just gets me excited. The Holy Spirit gives me inner joy and peace. He gradually empowers me in my daily prayers, handling temptations, trials, and tribulation as a Christian. I know that my strength comes from my heavenly Father and not by my might or flesh.

"You, dear children, are from God and have overcome them, because the one who is in you is greater than the one who is in the world." (1 John 4:4)

The Holy Spirit knows our weaknesses and helps us overcome every challenge to become victorious like Jesus. We stumble but we are not utterly cast away which is the essence of the sanctification process. We cannot carry out the Christian walk in the flesh but by being led or empowered by the person of the Holy Spirit. He wants to anoint our spiritual eyes so we can see the evil schemes that the devil has planned for us. The devil knows the power that we have in Christ and he is not going to fold his hands and let us get it. He is aware that when you discover your identity in Christ you are free indeed *(John 8:36).*

I share this testimony because I want to share the gift of love that I experienced when I got baptized by the Holy Spirit. I know that since God blessed me with this gift, He will surely bless you with it too. Confess your sins, accept Jesus Christ as your personal Lord and Savior, and go further to get baptized by immersion. God loves us the way we are and He is ready to accept us regardless of our past, if only we are ready to accept Him! We have a choice due to the free will God has given us.

"Behold, I stand at the door, and knock: if any man hear my voice, and open the door, I will come in to him, and will sup with him, and he with me." (Revelation 3:20)

The power of the Holy Spirit is available to us all and it is at the tip of our tongues, if we confess our sins. Proverbs 18:21 says *"Death and life are in the power of the tongue..."* What do you choose? Choose life today!

Our past experiences shape us to be what we are today, so it is not too late. I know some of us have already started our race, so keep running your race in Faith, Love and with Patience. The Lord's grace is sufficient for us all. As for me, after all these years I have spent on earth, I just realized that this is just my beginning. I cannot forget that experience. It was so real and personal. It was my own experience which God wants for everyone. It made me realize that the bible is real and I can experience what it says including what the apostles experienced. It showed me that I can have all the promises made to Abraham because I have received the Holy Spirit promised to everyone. *Oh, what a joy!* I have direct access to my heavenly Father.

"13 Christ hath redeemed us from the curse of the law, being made a curse for us: for it is written, Cursed is every one that hangeth on a tree: 14 That the blessing of Abraham might come on the Gentiles through Jesus Christ; that we might receive the promise of the Spirit through faith." *(Galatians 3:13-14)*

This scripture admonishes us that Christ died for us on the cross so that we may experience the promise of His Spirit through faith. We cannot doubt or be in unbelief, if we want to experience the fullness of God. Christ's resurrection from death signifies life. It provides the power necessary to bring all the dead areas of our lives to life. Our forgotten dreams can still be restored by His power. Our dream life begins to reveal more of God's plan for us. God begins to show us glimpses of our future. God's presence in our lives becomes much stronger. We are able to overcome in every area of our lives where we were once limited.

"And what is the exceeding greatness of his power to us-ward who believe, according to the working of his mighty power, Which he wrought in Christ, when he raised him from the dead, and set him at his own right hand in the heavenly places, Far above all principality, and power, and

might, and dominion, and every name that is named, not only in this world, but also in that which is to come." *(Ephesians 1:19-21)*

The Holy Spirit baptism was the promise that John, the Baptist proclaimed will happen as the forerunner of Jesus. John baptized the people by immersion in the Jordan River and spoke of the baptism of power by the Holy Spirit.

"I indeed baptize you with water unto repentance: but he that cometh after me is mightier than I, whose shoes I am not worthy to bear: he shall baptize you with the Holy Ghost, and with fire." (Matthew 3:11)

The sure way to receive spiritual blessings lies in your deep desire for them. There is a price to pay. You have to be open, yielded and hungry for the things of God. The Holy Spirit is gentle and will not force Himself on you. Ask God in prayer today for a deeper desire for your own experience through Jesus Christ. Ask God for the divine help of the Holy Spirit on this spiritual journey of life.

CHAPTER 5

3 in 1

> *"I will praise thee; for I am fearfully and
> wonderfully made: marvellous are thy
> works; and that my soul knoweth right
> well." (Psalm 139:14)*

L et us pause for a moment to go over some fundamental truths that will help us put some of the things discussed in the previous chapters in perspective. It will give us more insight as we go further into who we really are in Christ. Isn't it amazing to know that we are fearfully and wonderfully made? God has put so much thought into our creation and existence.

As mentioned in Psalm 139:14, we are fearfully and wonderfully made. Fearfully here means *"Power and Authority (dominion)"* and Wonderfully refers to the unique *"Gifts, Skills, and Talents"* that God has equipped us with to manifest here on earth and bring glory to His name. We are unique and God has hidden in every one of us "*Mysteries.*" These mysteries are divine codes about our lives which are divinely embedded in us to reveal our true identity of power, unique gifts and skills in Christ. We are to discover and uncover these mysteries on our personal journey toward an intimate relationship with God. Self-discovery is part of God's ultimate plan for us and we can only achieve this with the help of the Holy Spirit.

"*He hath made every thing beautiful in his time: also he hath set the world in their heart, so that no man can find out the work that God maketh from the beginning to the end.*" (*Ecclesiastes 3:11*)

Everything that we are and what we will become has already been placed in us from the foundation of this world. It had been settled before we were even formed in our mother's womb. You are not a mistake!

Everything that we are and what we will become has already been placed in us from the foundation of this world.

"*Before I formed thee in the belly I knew thee; and before thou camest forth out of the womb I sanctified thee, and I ordained thee a prophet unto the nations." (Jeremiah 1:5)*

We will dive deeper into the *divine nature of God*, the *Tripartite nature of Man* and the *Tabernacle of Moses*. We will discuss how they all unfold the divine plan that God has for humanity.

Trinity of the Godhead

"The distinct personalities of a Father, Son and Spirit."

Trinity is a Latin word *"Trinitas"* which means threefold. It is the belief that there is one God who eternally exists as three distinct persons (*the Father, Son, and Holy Spirit*).

The doctrine of Trinity has been confusing to many. As a science student, I will use *"Water"* to help explain it in such a manner that is understandable to all. Water exists in three distinct states: Solid, Liquid and Gas.

Solid: Water freezes to become ice at 0° Celsius, 32° Fahrenheit.

Liquid: Water is fluid at room temperature between 20 °C (68 °F) and 25 °C (77 °F). We are familiar with water in its liquid state.

Gas: Water exists as vapor in the air around us. You cannot see it. Water changes from liquid to gas or water vapor when boiled. Water can become gas at 100° C or 212 °F.

The molecules of water can exist in all three forms or states and this explains in simple way how our God exists as three distinct persons, yet still one God.

God, the Father loved the world that He sent His Son into the world that whosoever believes in Him will not perish but have everlasting life. His Son came to this world, was crucified, resurrected and returned to the Father. Also, the Father and the Son sent the Holy Spirit into the world to fulfil the promise Jesus made in John 14:26. This proves that God the Father, Son and the Holy Spirit are distinct from one another, yet there is only one God!

"But the Comforter, which is the Holy Ghost, whom the Father will send in my name, he shall teach you all things, and bring all things to your remembrance, whatsoever I have said unto you." (John 14:26)

Tripartite Nature of Man

"You are a spirit with a soul, living in a body."

God eternally exists as three distinct persons and it makes sense that they decided to create man with three parts. During the heavenly board meeting God had with Jesus and the Holy Spirit, they came up with a plan. They created man in their image and after their likeness as a tripartite being which means having or consisting of three parts.

"And God said, Let us make man in our image, after our likeness..." (Genesis 1:26a).

From scripture, we can deduce that *"Man"* consists of three parts, which are: Spirit, Soul and Body.

"And the very God of peace sanctify you wholly; and I pray God your whole spirit and soul and body be preserved blameless unto the coming of our Lord Jesus Christ." (1 Thessalonians 5:23).

Our tripartite nature emphasizes and proves that we are fearfully and wonderfully made. We are 3 in 1. We have three powerful natures packaged into one. We are a spirit having a soul, living in a body. We are spiritual beings having a human experience here on earth which Jesus exemplified when He came to earth. We are in this world but not of this world. We are divinely loaded with so much untapped potential, yet to be explored or even discovered.

"But we have this treasure in earthen vessels, that the excellency of the power may be of God, and not of us." *(2 Corinthians 4:7)*

Our duty is to have an understanding of our tripartite nature in order to live a victorious Christian life. God created the earth and has given man a spirit, with a soul and body to adapt and survive in it. God created us in such a way that our spirit is able to connect with His Spirit. With this powerful spiritual union, man has been given authority by God to use the spirit to rule the soul and the body, thereby exercising dominion over the earth.

"And God said, Let us make man in our image, after our likeness: and let them have dominion over the fish of the sea, and over the fowl of the air, and over the cattle, and over all the earth, and over every creeping thing that creepeth upon the earth." *(Genesis 1:26)*

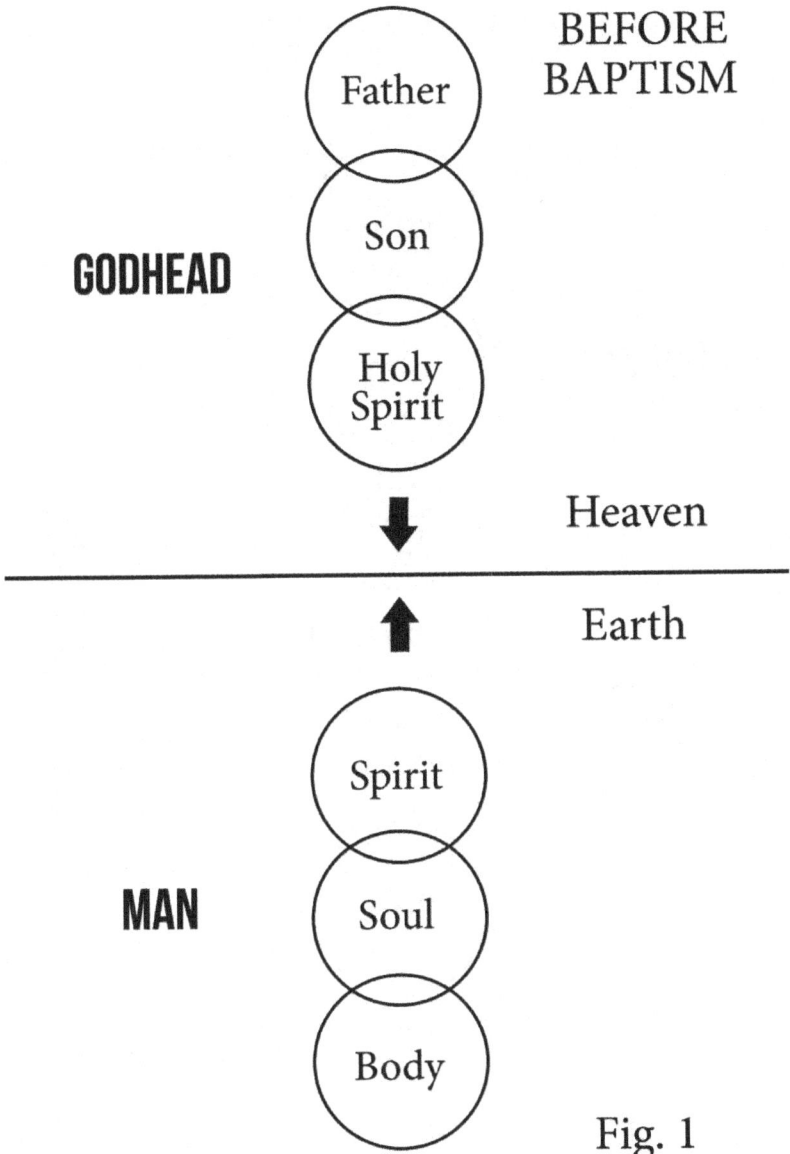

Fig. 1

AFTER BAPTISM

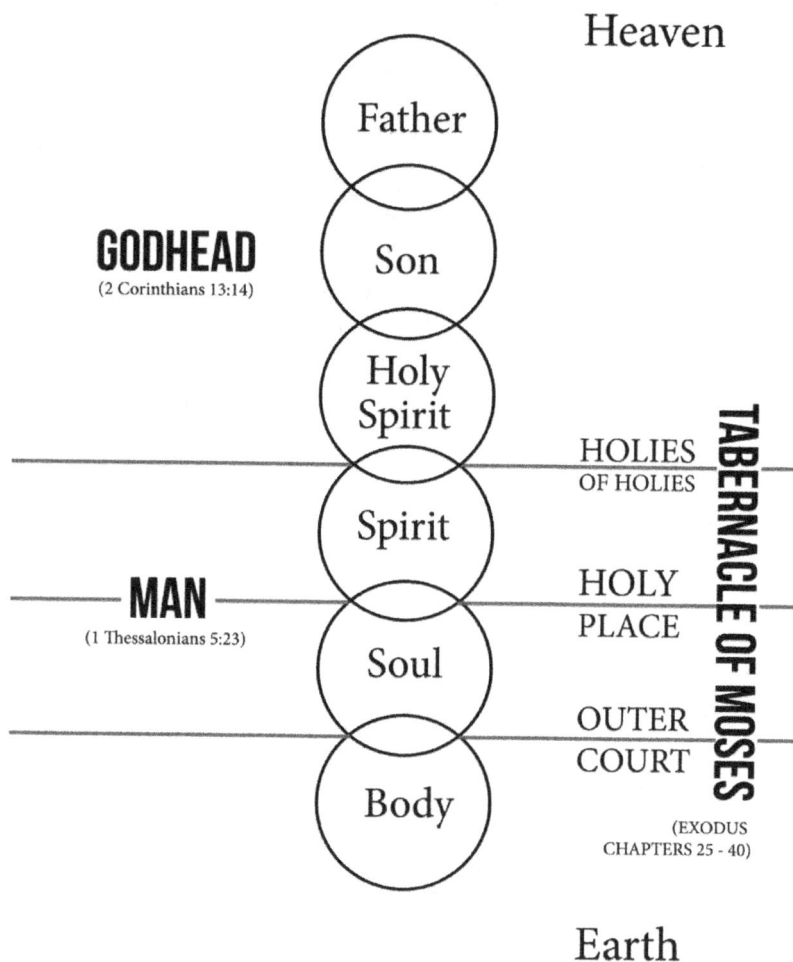

Heaven

GODHEAD
(2 Corinthians 13:14)

Father

Son

Holy
Spirit

HOLIES
OF HOLIES

Spirit

MAN
(1 Thessalonians 5:23)

HOLY
PLACE

Soul

Body

OUTER
COURT

TABERNACLE OF MOSES

(EXODUS
CHAPTERS 25 - 40)

Earth

Fig. 2

The Human Spirit

The human spirit (also referred to as our *"inner man"* or as *"spirit"* with a lower case *"s"*) is the part of man that makes us God-conscious or aware of God's presence. God gave us a spirit to experience Him. In man's unfallen state in the Garden of Eden, the human spirit of Adam and Eve were illuminated by God, and they enjoyed an intimate relationship with Him.

"And they heard the voice of the Lord God walking in the garden in the cool of the day: and Adam and his wife hid themselves from the presence of the Lord God amongst the trees of the garden." (Genesis 3:8)

However, that intimate relationship was broken when they were deceived by the serpent. As shown in Fig. 1, there is a separation between the Holy Spirit and our human spirit. Sin created a veil or separation between our spirit and the presence of God. As shown in Fig. 2, the spirit man represents the *Holies of Holies*. We can observe that our spirit is the part of us that communicates directly with the Holy Spirit. It is the part that gets illuminated with light and revelation by the Holy Spirit so that we can experience the power of the new life in Christ. The human spirit is the real you and it is the part of man that is regenerated when you give your life to Christ.

"The spirit of man is the candle of the Lord, searching all the inward parts of the belly." (Proverbs 20:27)

It is our human spirit that the Holy Spirit reveals our true and divine identity. He tells our spirit that we are children of God and keeps reminding us that we belong to God. Our spirit then passes on the information to the soul.

"The Spirit itself beareth witness with our spirit, that we are the children of God." (Romans 8:16)

Upon death, a believer's spirit is the part of man that leaves the body and goes to heaven for eternity.

"Then shall the dust return to the earth as it was: and the spirit shall return unto God who gave it."
(Ecclesiastes 12:7)

The human spirit is the most vital part of your Christian walk. You cannot receive or experience anything spiritual without your spirit man. Your spirit man is the one directly in contact with the spirit realm. The contact with the spirit realm can be either glorious or demonic. It is essential to guard what you allow into our spirit.

"9 But as it is written, Eye hath not seen, nor ear heard, neither have entered into the heart of man, the things which God hath prepared for them that love him. 10 But God hath

revealed them unto us by his Spirit: for the Spirit searcheth all things, yea, the deep things of God. 11 For what man knoweth the things of a man, save the spirit of man which is in him? even so the things of God knoweth no man, but the Spirit of God. 12 Now we have received, not the spirit of the world, but the spirit which is of God; that we might know the things that are freely given to us of God. 13 Which things also we speak, not in the words which man's wisdom teacheth, but which the Holy Ghost teacheth; comparing spiritual things with spiritual." (1 Corinthians 2:9-13)

Amazing! The Holy Spirit reveals to our spirit things that we cannot see with our natural eyes, or hear with our natural ears or things we have not yet thought about. There are numerous thoughts and ideas in God yet to be expressed or invented today. You may have heard believers talk about having dreams and visions of God or of heaven. They have experienced the spirit realm by their spirit. The Holy Spirit is the one responsible for revealing God's plans to our spirit man. The Holy Spirit searches through all the plans in heaven until He finds those that concern you and then reveals them to your spirit *(it can be in form of visions, trances, and dreams)* which is why He is referred to as our "helper". He desires to lead us, teach us and comfort us if we are sensitive to the witness of our spirit man.

Many of us are not even aware of this spiritual truth. Jesus Christ spoke a lot about the spirit realm when He discussed with the Pharisees and even His disciples. However, they were spiritually blind and could not comprehend most of what He said. They interpreted most of His words with their intellect. God gave us a spirit in order to connect with us, to fellowship and to have an intimate relationship with Him. For this reason, every human being has an affinity for spiritual things.

Most of what we know about the spirit realm is usually what we may have read or watched in movies about psychic activity, magic shows, new age religion or activities involving occultism such as witchcraft or consulting Ouija boards. In the book of Exodus, God told Moses to place his staff on the ground and it turned into a snake. Have we wondered why Moses fled when he saw the snake? Most shepherds protect their sheep from snakes by killing them or chasing them away. However, Moses who had lived in Egypt had seen magicians turn staffs to snakes and control them at will in the palace, so he fled. Moses saw this type of display first in the Egyptian palace before He saw God perform it by the burning bush. The devil never creates anything but likes to pervert what God has created so that people question and reject them. The devil does this in order to produce confusion, fear and doubt so that even believers in the church will reject them. Sadly, this is one of the reasons why topics about the spirit realm, speaking in tongues or the person of the Holy Spirit are considered weird or spooky.

Like Moses, our initial exposure to spiritual practices and principles has been perverted by the devil. As a result, we reject the spiritual principles that will enable us experience the spiritual realm in Christ. Today, we do not see the display of power as God intended for the church due to this perversion by the devil. However, God still has a divine plan to reveal this wisdom and expose the powers of darkness to the churches in the body of Christ.

"To the intent that now unto the principalities and powers in heavenly places might be known by the church the manifold wisdom of God." (Ephesians 3:10)

As a young boy, I always wondered what was behind the clouds in the sky. I observed the clouds and sometimes wondered *"If the clouds were removed and we could have a glimpse of heaven, what would we see?"* We seek and yearn to know or experience the spiritual realm because God wired us that way when He breathed into our body the breath of life, *called our spirit man!*

"And the Lord God formed man of the dust of the ground, and breathed into his nostrils the breath of life; and man became a living soul." (Genesis 2:7)

This is the reason why every human being despite our differences in religion is seeking after God, our creator. We are to treat our spirit with uttermost care. We cannot understand the things of God without our human spirit.

"But there is a spirit in man: and the inspiration of the Almighty giveth them understanding." (Job 32:8)

The spirit man is the part that first receives an encounter with God when we give our life to Christ and get baptized by immersion or filled with the Holy Spirit. Also, it is the first place we are attacked by satanic forces.

"The spirit of a man will sustain his infirmity; but a wounded spirit who can bear?" (Proverbs 18:14)

Our spirit cooperates with the Holy Spirit to pray effectively and according to the will of God. Our spirit is eager to partner with the Holy Spirit to pray for us if we yield ourselves to pray in tongues. These prayers are offered on your behalf by your spirit according to God's perfect plan for your life.

"And he that searcheth the hearts knoweth what is the mind of the Spirit, because he maketh intercession for the saints according to the will of God." (Romans 8:27)

"Praying always with all prayer and supplication in the Spirit, and watching thereunto with all perseverance and supplication for all saints." (Ephesians 6:18)

It is the spirit man that cooperates with the Holy Spirit and gets strengthened in prayer when we pray in tongues. Power and love flows through the Holy Spirit to our spirit as we connect to God's presence in prayer.

"That he would grant you, according to the riches of his glory, to be strengthened with might by his Spirit in the inner man." (Ephesians 3:16)

The Holies of Holies is our *"Promised land"* as believers. Our spirit and the Holy Spirit are meant to be united in order to get to this destination. This is the place of rest and purpose reserved for every believer. We can only get there by mixing the word of God with faith. This is the promise of rest spoken about in chapter 4 of the book of Hebrews:

"Let us therefore fear, lest, a promise being left us of entering into his rest, any of you should seem to come short of it.

*2 For unto us was the gospel preached, as well as unto them:
but the word preached did not profit them, not being mixed
with faith in them that heard it." (Hebrews 4:1-2)*

Your Divine Nature and Attributes (*DNA*) which includes your spiritual office, gifts of the Spirit and fruit of the Spirit are stored in your spirit man from the time God thought of you, formed you and placed you in your mother's womb. No one can give you anything that God has not already placed within you. All you need and all that you are has been divinely placed within you to discover and use to fulfil your purpose.

*"Neither shall they say, Lo here! or, lo there! for, behold, the
kingdom of God is within you." (Luke 17:21)*

Therefore, no man or woman formed by God and born into this world should ever think of accepting as a fact that he or she is a mistake or without purpose! You are already wired with a divine purpose which can only be revealed to your spirit when you have an encounter with the Holy Spirit. He is the *"promise of rest"* that Jesus told the disciples about before He ascended to heaven.

Once we yield our spirit to the Holy Spirit we experience the spirit realm and are able to do exploits. It is the part that gives us the capacity or power to do the work of God. Our spirit is designed to receive strength from the Holy Spirit. The spiritual gifts from God are deposited in our spirit and activated or revived by the measure of the power of the Holy Spirit that our spirit is exposed to and what our spirit can retain.

"Now unto him that is able to do exceeding abundantly above all that we ask or think, according to the power that worketh in us." (Ephesians 3:20)

The strength of our spirit man is directly proportional to the power at work in our spirit. It is out of this union with our spirit *(and the capacity that our spirit can handle)* that the power of the Holy Spirit flows to do His work. Our spirit is like the vessel or plumb line that the power of God flows through to do His work. In Physics class, we were taught that conductors allow electrical current flow through it to supply power. God desires that our spirit become like pure conductors to allow a free flow of power from Him to us to fulfil our divine purpose.

"He that believeth on me, as the scripture hath said, out of his belly shall flow rivers of living water." (John 7:38)

It is important to note that sin prevents the flow of God's power through us. In Physics, an insulator does not allow electrical current flow through it *(Romans 6:23)*. Sin acts like an insulator preventing the free flow of God's power in our lives. In order to keep flowing in the power of God, we have to deliberately avoid sin and continuously nurture our spirit man with the word of God and fervent prayers.

The Human Soul

The soul consists of the mind, will, and emotion. The soul is located between the spirit and the body. There is a constant battle between the spirit and the body to control the soul. The soul is the part of man that gets developed when we attain great academic achievements in the world such as those achieved by Doctors, Lawyers, Architects, Engineers and Accountants. Scientists have had great breakthroughs in the study of the ocean, animals, planet earth, human body, plant life, technology, atmosphere, outer space, and living organisms. These breakthroughs acknowledged by the world are from the soul's great desire to seek for knowledge. Our ***intellect*** is stimulated by these achievements and we enjoy temporary fulfilment from the rewards that come with these knowledge and breakthroughs.

"But thou, O Daniel, shut up the words, and seal the book, even to the time of the end: many shall run to and fro, and knowledge shall be increased." (Daniel 12:4)

As declared in this scripture, we observe that there is an increase in information today. It is our soul that houses and processes the information we need to develop our natural skills and talents. This information is used based on the way our bodies are created by God. We may observe that there are family traits that run down our lineage. As believers, we have been conditioned to acknowledge *"Generational Curses"* and pay little or no attention to the numerous *"Generational Blessings"* that we may have inherited too. If we study Abraham, Isaac and Jacob, we will observe common traits and similar occurrence of events in their lives.

If we take some time to do a little research on our family background, we will observe certain dominant talents, skills and abilities that we may have trivialized but inherited from our predecessors. Shortly after I gave my life to Christ, as I studied the bible, I observed the similarities in some families mentioned in the bible such as that of Abraham, Isaac and Jacob. I took some time to develop an excel spreadsheet and began to populate my family tree. I asked questions about my predecessors and findings were amazing! There were skills and talents that I realized I had inherited from my predecessors.

We may discover that our love to build things, write, dance, sing, play a certain type of sport, craftiness with our hands, or our love for numbers are generational traits. God does not waste resources. All God has put in us are designed to help us fulfil our divine assignment and purpose. Our duty is to discover them. These distinct and unique generational blessings are housed in our soul and can be passed down from one generation to another although some traits may skip one or two generations. As a believer, the Spirit of God enhances those skills or talents for His purpose and to be a blessing to others. Bezalel and Oholiab were examples of skilled craftsmen who God enhanced their skills to help Moses build the tabernacle *(Exodus 36:1)*.

The soul houses our **emotions** when we cry, laugh, get angry, anxious, excited, worry, or sad.

"Therefore I will not refrain my mouth; I will speak in the anguish of my spirit; I will complain in the bitterness of my soul." (Job 7:11)

As shown in Fig. 2, the Soul represents the *Holy Place.* As believers, when the word of God comes into our soul, our **mind** becomes stretched and renewed with the new and divine information received. The pattern of information that comes into our mind from this world is that of fear, anxiety and doubt. The mind is renewed by trying to assimilate and adjust to the information of faith which is the pleasing and perfect will of God for our lives.

"And be not conformed to this world: but be ye transformed by the renewing of your mind, that ye may prove what is that good, and acceptable, and perfect, will of God." *(Romans 12:2)*

As we practice meditating on the word our mind is renewed. Our mind is the place where the battle takes place. It is located in our soul between the spirit and the body. The word of God renews the mind by replacing it with the old information giving it rest and peace once it is renewed regarding that situation. The information is stored up and used again toward a similar situation.

"Casting down imaginations, and every high thing that exalteth itself against the knowledge of God, and bringing into captivity every thought to the obedience of Christ." *(2 Corinthians 10:5)*

"Truly my soul waiteth upon God: from him cometh my salvation." *(Psalm 62:1)*

"Thou wilt keep him in perfect peace, whose mind is stayed on thee: because he trusteth in thee." (Isaiah 26:3)

Our **will** (commonly referred to as "Willpower") is what gives us the drive to go on in life during adversity. When we surrender our will to the word of God we accomplish much for the kingdom. Jesus Christ had to surrender His will to the will of the Father when He said *"not My will but Your will be done" (Luke 22:42)*. Our will is our determination to do something difficult whether good or bad. This is why we have to be filled with God's word to know God's perfect will and then surrender our will to the revelation of His will for every situation. We surrender to God's will out of our great love for Him.

"Jesus said unto him, Thou shalt love the Lord thy God with all thy heart, and with all thy soul, and with all thy mind." (Matthew 22:37)

The Human Body

We are very familiar with our body also referred to as *"the flesh."* We have been conscious of its existence from the time we were born. As shown in Fig. 2, our body represents the *Outer Court*. It is the part of man that is in contact with the earth. We eat, sleep, shower and dress it up daily. Most of all that we do involves our body. Our body deals with the five senses of sight, hearing, smell, taste and touch. The body is the vessel or home for our soul and spirit. Once our spirit leaves our body, it means that we are dead. It is buried, then decays and becomes dust. God has given everyone a spirit with a soul to live in a body over an average period of eighty years to accomplish our purpose here on earth.

"10 The days of our years are threescore years and ten; and if by reason of strength they be fourscore years, yet is their strength labour and sorrow; for it is soon cut off, and we fly away." (Psalm 90:10)

The body has a lot of desires for things of this world because it is the part of man that is directly in contact with the world. We are required to take care of our body but not let it rule us. For this reason, we need to control our desires. The body contends with the spirit to control the soul. The body usually wins the battle when the spirit man is not regenerated and strengthened by the Holy Spirit.

Today, we realize that most of what we do is for the body. As a follower of Christ, we quickly realize that the body needs to be controlled. The body craves for food when it is time to fast or the body craves for sleep when it is time to pray. The body does not desire to be put under any type of spiritual exercise because it will be denied its pleasures. The body loves freedom and has a tendency to be wild so it needs to the tamed or disciplined. Athletes discipline their bodies to achieve their goals. They prepare their bodies for competition on strict diets and vigorous exercises to win a prize. Paul made some notable remarks about this in relation to his life as a believer:

"But I keep under my body, and bring it into subjection: lest that by any means, when I have preached to others, I myself should be a castaway." (1 Corinthians 9:27)

"22 For I delight in the law of God after the inward man: 23 But I see another law in my members, warring against the law of my mind, and bringing me into captivity to the law of sin which is in my members. 24 O wretched man that I am! who shall deliver me from the body of this death? 25 I thank God through Jesus Christ our Lord. So then with the mind I myself serve the law of God; but with the flesh the law of sin." (Romans 7:22-25)

We are to acknowledge our weaknesses before the Lord in prayer and ask for grace and strength daily. With the new life in Christ, there should be a plan to overcome the desires of the body. Paul said that there was a constant battle between the soul and the body. You are to present yourself as a living sacrifice to God as your body is no longer yours. Your body is now a temple where God desires to reside.

"I have been crucified with Christ and I no longer live, but Christ lives in me. The life I now live in the body, I live by faith in the Son of God, who loved me and gave himself for me." (Galatians 2:20)

"I beseech you therefore, brethren, by the mercies of God, that ye present your bodies a living sacrifice, holy, acceptable unto God, which is your reasonable service." (Romans 12:1)

"Know ye not that ye are the temple of God, and that the Spirit of God dwelleth in you?" (1 Corinthians 3:16)

As mentioned in Chapter 3, fasting is a great way to discipline our bodies. We build control over our bodies when we abstain from food to seek God which is very rewarding. It is a rewarding experience to incorporate fasting into our weekly spiritual activity. We can set aside a day or two to fast each week to keep us spiritually fit. There are different types of fast. However, it is important to note that whichever type of fast you embark on, the goal of fasting is to draw closer to God. Daniel was an example of someone who benefited from fasting both physically and spiritually. The bible mentions that he looked physically better than his peers and was also rewarded with divine skills, wisdom, knowledge and understanding by God.

"And at the end of ten days their countenances appeared fairer and fatter in flesh than all the children which did eat the portion of the king's meat." (Daniel 1:15)

"As for these four children, God gave them knowledge and skill in all learning and wisdom: and Daniel had understanding in all visions and dreams. (Daniel 1:17)

Our bodies play a vital role in carrying out our divine assignment. We are custodians of our bodies and should take proper care of it by exercising, managing our emotions, eating healthy and getting enough rest. It is great to have our five or ten year plan but if we are not in good health it will be difficult to achieve them.

"Beloved, I wish above all things that thou mayest prosper and be in health, even as thy soul prospereth." (3 John 1:2)

Jesus Christ had a busy schedule and often went to the mountain top to pray, yet He took time to rest in the boat as He went about doing His Father's business. However, we should be mindful not to focus all our time and energy on our body without paying attention to what is going on with our spirit and soul.

Tabernacle of Moses

*"Our experience on the journey from the
Outer Court through the Holy Place to
the Holies of Holies."*

The tabernacle of Moses was the pattern God gave Moses for the Israelites to approach and experience Him. The divine pattern was also mentioned in Hebrews Chapter 9 and is relevant in our walk with God. It is essential to understand how it relates to our spiritual journey here on earth. Jesus came to make the physical tabernacle that Moses built, a spiritual experience. The tabernacle *(shown in Fig.3 on page 98)*, was described as having three courts which are the Outer Court, the Holy Place and the Holies of Holies.

The first court which is the *"Outer Court"* consists of the Altar of Burnt Offering and the Brazen Laver or Basin. It was the busiest and noisiest section of the tabernacle. It was the part that had the Israelites going in and out with animals offered as sacrifice for their sins.

The second court is the *"Holy Place"* which consists of the Golden Candlestick, the Table of Shewbread and the

Golden Altar of Incense. Priests go into the Holy Place to place twelve loaves of unleavened bread *(for each tribe of Israel)* on the Table of Shewbread. The Priests ate the bread inside the Holy Place every Sabbath and placed fresh loaves on the table. The Golden Candlestick lit up the room and the oil was kept filled to keep the light from going out. The Priests burnt incense every morning and evening at the Altar of Incense and the smoke from the incense filled the Holy of Holies through the veil.

The third court is the *"Holies of Holies"* which consists of the Veil, the Ark of the Covenant and the Mercy Seat. This part is the most sacred of the tabernacle. Once a year, on the Day of Atonement, the High Priest was permitted to enter the Holies of Holies to burn incense and sprinkle the blood of a sacrificial animal on the Mercy Seat of the Ark. The Priest atoned for his sins and those of the people of Israel by offering the sacrifice.

So far I have mentioned my Outer Court experience from Chapters 1 to 3. Our journey begins when we have a personal spiritual exodus from our sinful lifestyle. We have to make that decision to leave our old ways which has kept us as slaves *(state of living below our potential)* outside the tabernacle. We proceed with our journey into the Outer Court when we either respond to an altar call or when we decide to go before the Lord in confession and repentance of sin.

How does understanding the Godhead, the tripartite nature of man and the tabernacle of Moses affect our spiritual journey here on earth? I believe the Israelites asked the same question too? They did not comprehend the spiritual plan of God for their lives. They had lived in bondage all their lives. God's plan was to take them out of bondage and introduce them to a new way of life which was spiritual and needed much faith. Jesus Christ came to make the pattern of the Tabernacle of Moses a spiritual reality for everyone to experience.

"But Christ being come an high priest of good things to come, by a greater and more perfect tabernacle, not made with hands, that is to say, not of this building."
(Hebrew 9:11)

Today, Jesus stands as our High Priest and His blood was shed on the cross to take away the sacrifice of goats and bulls so that we can have our own personal experience of the Holies of Holies. Jesus is saying to you even right now as your High Priest:

"And the Spirit and the bride say, Come..."
(Revelation 22:17a)

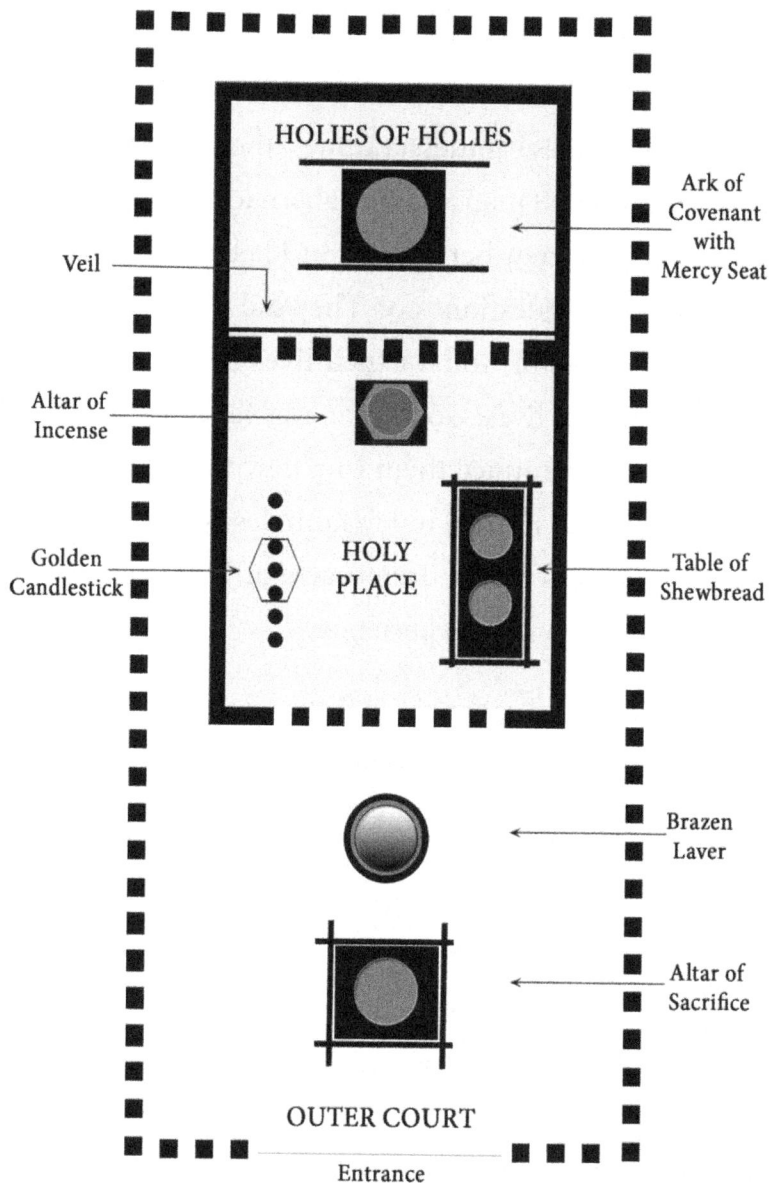

HOLIES OF HOLIES

Veil

Ark of
Covenant
with
Mercy Seat

Altar of
Incense

HOLY
PLACE

Golden
Candlestick

Table of
Shewbread

Brazen
Laver

Altar of
Sacrifice

OUTER COURT

Entrance

TABERNACLE OF MOSES Fig. 3

CHAPTER 6

Who is the Holy Spirit?

"The Holy Spirit is the person who empowers us. Without Him there are no greater works!"

In the Tabernacle of Moses, the Golden Candlestick *(located in the Holy Place)* represents the Holy Spirit. Like a candle, the Holy Spirit enlightens and illuminates, creating lots of *"lightbulb moments"* in our lives. As we have mentioned in earlier chapters, the Holy Spirit is the person of the Trinity who empowers and equips us to do the work of God.

Generally, we have heard people refer to Him as wind, it, water, fire, or anointing. However, the Holy Spirit is a person and is referred to as *"He"*, *"Holy Spirit"* or *"Spirit"* with a capital *"S"* in the bible. Jesus Christ promised that when He leaves to be with the Father, He will send us someone like Him to be with us and help us.

"And I will pray the Father, and he shall give you another Comforter, that he may abide with you for ever." (John 14:16)

"And when he is come, he will reprove the world of sin, and of righteousness, and of judgment." (John 16:8)

God sent us the Holy Spirit as a way of fulfilling the covenant He made with Abraham when He promised to bless him and his descendants *(which includes us).* We can only redeem or lay claim to the blessings of God's covenant with Abraham through receiving the first promise, which is in the person of Holy Spirit.

"13 Christ hath redeemed us from the curse of the law, being made a curse for us: for it is written, Cursed is every one that hangeth on a tree: 14 That the blessing of Abraham might come on the Gentiles through Jesus Christ; that we might receive the promise of the Spirit through faith." (Galatians 3:13-14)

All our inheritance in Christ is distributed to us by the Holy Spirit so we have to get to know Him.

All our divine inheritance in Christ is distributed to us by the Holy Spirit so we have to get to know Him.

Proverbs 13:22 says *"A good man leaveth an inheritance to his children's children..."* Also, Paul talked about our inheritance in the letter he wrote to the church in Ephesus when he prayed that they will receive the riches of the glory of their inheritance in Christ *(Ephesians 1:18).* We cannot explore the spiritual blessings God has for us without the Holy Spirit.

The Holy Spirit was there when the earth was created. He provided the creative power needed during creation.

"And the earth was without form, and void; and darkness was upon the face of the deep. And the Spirit of God moved upon the face of the waters." (Genesis 1:2)

The Holy Spirit has emotions and can be grieved.

"And grieve not the holy Spirit of God, whereby ye are sealed unto the day of redemption." (Ephesians 4:30)

The Holy Spirit is the person who makes our Christian walk exciting and adventurous. Without Him there will be no greater works. He empowers us to do the greater works Jesus promised that we would do before He ascended to heaven, after being resurrected by the Holy Spirit.

"But ye shall receive power, after that the Holy Ghost is come upon you: and ye shall be witnesses unto me both in Jerusalem, and in all Judaea, and in Samaria, and unto the uttermost part of the earth." (Acts 1:8)

"Then he answered and spake unto me, saying, This is the word of the Lord unto Zerubbabel, saying, Not by might, nor by power, but by my spirit, saith the Lord of hosts." (Zechariah 4:6)

The person of the Holy Spirit has been mostly misunderstood partly because He is not seen or we think He is spooky. We become frightened when we refer to Him as *"Holy Spirit"* or *"Holy Ghost."* In many churches, the message of the Holy Spirit or speaking in tongues is not even discussed or accepted. It is the devil's plan to keep this revelation out of the church. Without the Holy Spirit, there is no power.

"But as many as received him, to them gave he power to become the sons of God, even to them that believe on his name." (John 1:12)

We may have been Christians for many years and still have no relationship with Jesus or the Holy Spirit. However, the Holy Spirit is the person that reveals who we are in Christ. He assures us that we are children of God. It is quite comforting to know that there were some believers in the bible who did not know the Holy Spirit until they met Paul, who told them about Him.

"1 And it came to pass, that, while Apollos was at Corinth, Paul having passed through the upper coasts came to Ephesus: and finding certain disciples, 2 He said unto them, Have ye received the Holy Ghost since ye believed? And they said unto him, We have not so much as heard whether there be any Holy Ghost." (Acts 19:1-2)

As we read further, we discover that Paul prayed for them and they were baptized and filled with the Holy Spirit.

"5 When they heard this, they were baptized in the name of the Lord Jesus. 6 And when Paul had laid his hands upon them, the Holy Ghost came on them; and they spake with tongues, and prophesied." (Acts 19:5-6)

I have heard people ask *"Which comes first, baptism by immersion or the Holy Spirit baptism?"* From studying the bible, we observe that it can happen in any order as God wills. Most people usually get baptized by immersion before being baptized by the Holy Spirit since that was the way it was presented to them. However, you can also experience the Holy Spirit baptism if the opportunity presents itself like what happened in the home of a man named Cornelius.

"44 While Peter yet spake these words, the Holy Ghost fell on all them which heard the word. 45 And they of the circumcision which believed were astonished, as many as came with Peter, because that on the Gentiles also was poured out the gift of the Holy Ghost. 46 For they heard them speak with tongues, and magnify God. Then answered Peter, 47 Can any man forbid water, that these should not be baptized, which have received the Holy Ghost as well as we? 48 And he commanded them to be baptized in the name of the Lord. Then prayed they him to tarry certain days." (Acts 10:44-48)

We observe that they received the Holy Spirit baptism before they were later baptized by immersion. Once we have been baptized by immersion and filled with the Holy Spirit with evidence of speaking in tongues, our lives should never remain the same. The person of the Holy Spirit is revealed to us as we begin a relationship with Him. He is the person who reveals our identity, purpose and divine assignment in Christ.

He knows all things and gives us great insight into how we fit in the divine plan of God. Paul wrote his letters *(called "Epistles")* to the numerous churches, John wrote the book of Revelation in the Island of Patmos, Ezekiel was taken and shown things that were happening in the temple, Moses wrote the first five books of the bible *(called the "Torah" in Hebrew)*. All these and much more were done with the help of the Holy Spirit.

"9 But as it is written, Eye hath not seen, nor ear heard, neither have entered into the heart of man, the things which God hath prepared for them that love him. 10 But God hath revealed them unto us by his Spirit: for the Spirit searcheth all things, yea, the deep things of God."
(1 Corinthians 2:9-10)

The Holy Spirit equips us to do the unique work God has created us to do. He gives us spiritual gifts for this purpose as He wills, as stated in 1 Corinthians 12:7 -11:

"7 But the manifestation of the Spirit is given to every man to profit withal. 8 For to one is given by the Spirit the word of wisdom; to another the word of knowledge by the same Spirit; 9 To another faith by the same Spirit; to another the gifts of healing by the same Spirit; 10 To another the working of miracles; to another prophecy; to another discerning of spirits; to another divers kinds of tongues; to another the interpretation of tongues: 11 But all these

worketh that one and the selfsame Spirit, dividing to every man severally as he will."

God so loved the world that He sent His Son Jesus to die on the cross for us. However, part of the plan was revealed when Jesus told his disciples that He was going back to His Father after resurrection. He mentioned that God was going to send us another comforter who will help us here on earth and be with us forever.

The role of the Holy Spirit in our lives is very dynamic. Jesus promised that the Holy Spirit will come to teach us *(John 14:26),* testify about God to us *(John 15:26),* guide us *(Romans 8:14),* convict us of sin *(John 16:8),* speak to us *(1 Corinthians 2:13),* enlighten us about the word *(John 16:13),* intercede for us *(Romans 8:26),* empower us *(Acts 1:8),* comfort us (John 16:7), led us in all truth *(John 16:13),* glorify God *(John 16:14),* led us into purpose *(Luke 4:1),* reveal dreams and visions *(Joel 2:28)* and help us in every area of our lives *(John 14:26).*

The power of the Holy Ghost is God's gift to the church as Christ promised. It is the resurrection power that is available to all those who ask for it. How do we know it is available? Christ instructed His disciples after His death and resurrection, to wait in prayer for power from heaven. This promise came to them as the baptism of the Holy Ghost which happened on the day of Pentecost.

The Holy Spirit is the one who introduces us to the spirit realm. Many religions try in their own ways to get to God. Jesus said He will send another helper that will remind us about all that He did. Jesus knew that we will never be able to understand, remember or achieve all that He had done here on earth without a supernatural helper.

"Everything the Father has is Mine. This is why I told you that He (the Holy Spirit) takes from what is Mine and will declare it to you." (John 16:15)

As believers, the Holy Spirit is the *only* person that can introduce us to the spirit realm in order to experience the supernatural which includes having visions, trances and dreams. It is important to note that any other means or medium is *not* of God. He provides the power necessary for us to operate in our gifting and ministry. It was the Holy Spirit who led Jesus Christ into His ministry.

"And Jesus being full of the Holy Ghost returned from Jordan, and was led by the Spirit into the wilderness." (Luke 4:1)

The Holy Spirit supplies the power needed to fulfill our purpose. He gives us strength to accomplish our daily tasks without being burnt out. He energizes and refills us daily after we accept Christ and get baptized. Like the early disciples, it is through the power of the Holy Spirit that we can effectively carry out our service to God. We can now pray effectively, have boldness to witness to others, overcome our daily struggles, and be conformed to the image of Christ. We know that without Christ we can do nothing. It is only through the power of the Holy Spirit that we can attain the higher calling of God and accomplish what God has in mind for us.

Our mission on earth is not only to receive salvation and stop there but to receive power from Christ through the Holy Spirit who will enable us impact the world. The disciples are spoken of in the bible today because of the promise of this power which they received on the day of Pentecost. We can pray fervently with passion, zeal and hunger for the same power of the Holy Ghost which is available to all who ask for it. Are you determined to be *"on fire"* for God? If not, why not? Get to know the Holy Spirit and the world will come to see you burn with His power!

CHAPTER 7

Solitude

"How we spend our time matters to God, especially time spent in His presence."

Time is valuable and priceless. Today, our world appears to be so fast paced. There is a high demand for our time considering all the tasks we need to accomplish each day. We are left with this feeling that there is never enough time in the day even though we all are given twenty-four hours. God expects us to spend quality time with Him despite our busy schedules.

"So teach us to number our days, that we may apply our hearts unto wisdom." (Psalm 90:12)

"I love them that love me; and those that seek me early shall find me." (Proverbs 8:17)

We are accountable for our time here on earth. God requires that we manage our time wisely. How we spend

our time is critical in relation
to our spiritual growth, our
intimacy with God and how
much impact we will make
here on earth. Paul talked
about redeeming the time

God expects us to
spend quality time
with Him despite our
busy schedules.

because the days we live in are evil. (Ephesians 5:16). We
can only redeem the time we have lost by spending quality
time with God. Time spent in God's presence studying His
word and in prayer is not a waste of time but very
rewarding. It is like the air we breathe. It gives a believer
life. Just as plants need water to grow so does time spent
with God nourish and refresh our spiritual lives.

"35 And in the morning, rising up a great while before day,
he went out, and departed into a solitary place, and there
prayed. 36 And Simon and they that were with him followed
after him. 37 And when they had found him, they said unto
him, All men seek for thee." (Mark 1:35-37)

Solitude means *deliberately* separating ourselves
from our busy schedules and techy gadgets to spend
quality time with God. This summarizes what takes place
in the "*Holy Place*" in the tabernacle of Moses. It is great to
have scheduled time away on personal retreats to seek God

during the day and each year. We can take daily prayer walks and schedule time away on personal retreats to seek God just as we schedule our vacation time away with our family and friends. We should deliberately schedule times when we will not be disturbed or distracted to seek God first in all our ways *(Matthew 6:33)*. Each year since I gave my life to Christ, I have scheduled time away to seek the face of God. It has been a rewarding decision and a time I look forward to each year. Jacob did this in Genesis 32:24 which says *"And Jacob was left alone; and there wrestled a man with him until the breaking of the day."* God gave him a new identity after this encounter. God blessed Jacob and changed his name to Israel during his time of solitude.

The Word

> *"The word of God is meant to be studied knowing that what we have read can be experienced."*

In the tabernacle of Moses, the Table of Shewbread *(located in the Holy Place)* represents the *"Word of God."* Manuals are provided for every product to guide the buyer on how to properly operate the product. The word of God *(the Bible)* is the manual for every believer. It is the foundation for every Christian. The words in the Bible are inspired by God and can be applied in our everyday life.

"All scripture is given by inspiration of God, and is profitable for doctrine, for reproof, for correction, for instruction in righteousness." (2 Timothy 3:16)

The word of God is the perfect will and mind of God for our lives. It is very important that we study the word of God for ourselves like the Berean believers. We should ensure that we get daily revelation from God's word for ourselves.

"These were more noble than those in Thessalonica, in that they received the word with all readiness of mind, and searched the scriptures daily, whether those things were so." (Acts 17:11)

We are required to meditate on the word of God daily when we study, according to Joshua 1:8. Meditation involves pausing to process what has been read. Anytime I think of meditation, I remember the illustration I learnt about cows *"chewing their cud"* from Agricultural Science class in High School. Have you ever noticed that they always seem to be chewing something? Cows chew their food twice in order to digest it properly. Their stomach has compartments where food is stored for later while grazing so that they can chew their cud to properly digest their food. Cows spend about eight hours every day chewing their cud. This method of chewing the cud to aid digestion is the definition of meditating on the word like the Berean Christians did. They took time to search the word of God after listening to Paul's sermons for better understanding and personal revelation of the word. Like the Berean believers, it is our duty to prove the words preached at our local churches. We can do this by searching the scriptures during our private study for personal understanding and revelation of the words preached.

"These were more noble than those in Thessalonica, in that they received the word with all readiness of mind, and searched the scriptures daily, whether those things were so." *(Acts 17:11)*

The word of God is the will and mind of God for every believer. We find purpose in His word. Jesus Christ found His assignment and purpose in the book of Isaiah *(Isaiah 61:1-3)*, as stated in book of Luke where it says:

"And there was delivered unto him the book of the prophet Esaias. And when he had opened the book, he found the place where it was written." *(Luke 4:17)*

The words in the bible are from God. God works in line with His word. God does nothing outside His word. In prayer, we are to remind God of what He said by confessing and declaring His word daily and in every situation.

"1 In the beginning was the Word, and the Word was with God, and the Word was God. 2 The same was in the beginning with God. 3 All things were made by him; and without him was not any thing made that was made." (John 1:1-3)

The words of God in the bible are promises made to us and are divine blessings written with the intent of enhancing our lives. In Ephesians 6:17, the word is referred to as the *"Sword"* of the spirit. As we study the word, we realize that it is so powerful that like a sword, it can go into our tripartite parts *(i.e. spirit, soul and body)* to separate what is of God from what is not of God. The word can be used to defeat the devil. The word of God helps us to discern what is from God and what is not from God.

"For the word of God is quick, and powerful, and sharper than any two edged sword, piercing even to the dividing asunder of soul and spirit, and of the joints and marrow, and is a discerner of the thoughts and intents of the heart." (Hebrews 4:12)

"And take the helmet of salvation, and the sword of the Spirit, which is the word of God." (Ephesians 6:17)

It is very essential for every believer to take time to study the word. Our spirit man grows stronger as we study the word daily. The more of the word we study, the more we grow in faith and full of the truth from God's word.

"Study to shew thyself approved unto God, a workman that needeth not to be ashamed, rightly dividing the word of truth." (2 Timothy 2:15)

The word of God is like a mirror *(James 1:23)*. Just as we look into the mirror to adjust our clothes, so is the word of God the mirror used to conform our identity to that of Christ. It is from the word that we realize that God has chosen us to minister before Him. God's perception of us is quite different from the way we perceive ourselves.

"But ye are a chosen generation, a royal priesthood, an holy nation, a peculiar people; that ye should shew forth the praises of him who hath called you out of darkness into his marvellous light." (1 Peter 2:9)

It is good practice to pray before we start reading the bible. We can ask the Holy Spirit to help us understand what we will be reading. We can pray against any form of distractions, for clarity of mind and for revelation of hidden secrets from the bible before we begin reading. The Holy Spirit will help to interpret what we have read in such a way that we can apply principles received from the word to our everyday lives.

"But the anointing which ye have received of him abideth in you, and ye need not that any man teach you: but as the same anointing teacheth you of all things, and is truth, and is no lie, and even as it hath taught you, ye shall abide in him." (1 John 2:27)

Today, there are numerous downloadable versions of the bible for our computers, phones and tablets. It can be helpful to study a bible version that you can easily understand. You can buy a study bible that has commentaries, outlines and a brief introduction to each book of the bible so you can read it in context. You can read up on topics that interest you to broaden your knowledge of how God relates with people in that area.

It is important to keep a realistic bible plan with more emphasis on reading to understand what the scriptures mean and how it can be applied in your life. As you study, you may find that you may be ruminating or meditation on the meaning of a scripture that jumps out at you for a couple of minutes or hours. It is good practice to have a notepad to write down some of your thoughts while studying and meditating on the word of God. Writing helps you to process your thoughts while you study. Also, you can attend bible study in your local church to get other believer's perspectives on subjects discussed from the bible.

It will be interesting to discover that someone at the bible study thinks the way you do on a particular subject.

Some helpful scriptures on Identity in Christ:
The Word of God says you are:

- forgiven – 1 John 1:9
- a joint heir with Christ – Romans 8:17
- loved – John 3:16
- in His thoughts and plan – Jeremiah 29:11
- a chosen generation – 1 Peter 2:9
- a personal witness of Christ – Acts 1:8
- gods *(with a small "g")* – John 10:34
- a new creature in Christ – 2 Corinthians 5:17
- a child of God – John 1:12
- fearfully and wonderfully made – Psalm 139:14
- engraved on the palm of His hands – Isaiah 49:16
- a citizen of heaven – Philippians 3:20
- a temple of God – 1 Corinthians 3:16

As we study the word daily, our desire to search deeper for more of the nourishment that will aid our spiritual growth should become greater. We begin to move from drinking milk to digesting the raw meat of the word.

"I have fed you with milk, and not with meat: for hitherto ye were not able to bear it, neither yet now are ye able."
(1 Corinthians 3:2)

A new born baby can only digest milk at birth. However, the baby will require solid foods to keep up with his or her growing body and increasing appetite. God desires that as we grow spiritually, we will begin to seek Him for deeper revelation of His word.

Prayer

> *"Speaking to God knowing that He not only listens but answers in a way that brings purpose and gives life."*

Prayer is God's idea. Prayer is part of God's plan to restore humanity back to what Adam and Eve enjoyed in the Garden of Eden. In the tabernacle of Moses, the *"Altar of Incense" (located in the Holy Place)* represents your *"Prayer life."* It was located right in front of the entrance of the Holies of Holies with the veil covering the entrance. The location of the altar is very important and lets us know that prayer brings us into the presence of God. God loves intimacy and has given us prayer as an avenue to have direct communication with Him.

"Call unto me, and I will answer thee, and show thee great and mighty things, which thou knowest not."
(Jeremiah 33:3)

Prayer is speaking, listening, speaking again, and then listening to God for answers. Prayer is not only offered on our knees but can be offered in many postures. We can pray to God while we are driving, doing chores, exercising and as we go about doing our business throughout the day. Prayer should become our lifestyle. Jesus is now our High Priest. His death and blood replaces the need for any mediator so we can go to God individually in prayer to pour out our hearts to Him. We can approach God freely in prayer as a child approaches a father.

As we make a habit of approaching God in prayer, we will come to know Him and draw ever nearer to Him. Our prayers will become what God desires and His angels will be empowered to carry out our requests. The angels of God respond to the word of God alone and are empowered by it. They carry out God's assignment based on the words in the bible that we confess, declare and decree in prayer.

"Bless the Lord, ye his angels, that excel in strength, that do his commandments, hearkening unto the voice of his word." (Psalm 103:20)

Studying the word helps us pray according to God's will for our lives. The Holy Spirit goes to the reservoir of the words we have studied and bring them to our minds to use in prayer for that situation according to God's will.

"If you abide in Me, and My words abide in you, you will ask what you desire, and it shall be done for you."
(John 15:7)

Faith is required in prayer. Our prayers are received and answered first in the spirit realm as we wait patiently with faith to receive the answers. We have to believe that we are praying to a God of Possibilities, who listens and answers our prayers. He created the heavens and the earth and everything in it. We cannot have doubt during and after prayer. Having faith when we pray pleases God.

"But without faith it is impossible to please him: for he that cometh to God must believe that he is, and that he is a rewarder of them that diligently seek him."
(Hebrews 11:6)

"Therefore I say unto you, What things soever ye desire, when ye pray, believe that ye receive them, and ye shall have them." (Mark 11:24)

The Veil
It is important to understand the significance of the veil as we discuss Prayer. In Hebrew, the word *"Veil"* means a divider, screen or separator that conceals. The veil was the curtain placed between the Holy Place and the Holies of Holies. The veil signifies the barrier created

between man and God when Adam and Eve sinned in the Garden and were sent out of it.

"23 Therefore the Lord God sent him forth from the garden of Eden, to till the ground from whence he was taken. 24 So he drove out the man; and he placed at the east of the garden of Eden Cherubims, and a flaming sword which turned every way, to keep the way of the tree of life." (Genesis 3:23-24)

A woman wears a veil during her wedding to conceal her face and beauty from her fiancé. Her face is concealed until after they have been pronounced husband and wife during the wedding ceremony. The veil in the tabernacle was a barrier put in place to make sure no one could carelessly enter into God's presence in an unclean state. The duty of the High Priest was to go into the Holies of Holies on the Day of Atonement to offer sacrifice for himself and for the sins committed by the Israelites in ignorance.

"But into the second went the high priest alone once every year, not without blood, which he offered for himself, and for the errors of the people." (Hebrews 9:7)

God had a plan to remove the veil to give access to everyone who desires to have an intimate relationship and enjoy His presence. God removed the requirement for anyone coming to Him on our behalf. This divine plan was accomplished when Jesus Christ died on the cross and the veil tore, as described in Matthew 27:50-51:

"50 Jesus, when he had cried again with a loud voice, yielded up the ghost. 51 And, behold, the veil of the temple was rent in twain from the top to the bottom; and the earth did quake, and the rocks rent."

What happened here is very significant for us to note as we study and engage in prayer. The veil in the temple tore from top to bottom considering the fact that it was very thick and its height was way too high for any individual to reach. It could only be an act of God and shows us that God desires that we all have access to Him. Today, we all have access to God and can approach Him in prayer by what Jesus did for us when He died on the cross, becoming our High Priest.

"Let us therefore come boldly unto the throne of grace, that we may obtain mercy, and find grace to help in time of need." (Hebrews 4:16)

"19 Which hope we have as an anchor of the soul, both sure and stedfast, and which entereth into that within the veil; 20 Whither the forerunner is for us entered, even Jesus, made an high priest for ever after the order of Melchisedec." (Hebrews 6:19-20)

One of the reasons Jesus said *"It is finished!"* on the cross was because what He did on the cross took away the old way of approaching God and established a new and living way for everyone to experience Him.

"By a new and living way, which he hath consecrated for us, through the veil, that is to say, his flesh." (Hebrews 10:20)
"I am the door: by me if any man enter in, he shall be saved, and shall go in and out, and find pasture." (John 10:9)

Now that we know we have access to the Father, we may ask ourselves *"How do I pray?"* The disciples asked Jesus to teach them how to pray. They examined His lifestyle and desired the same type of relationship and results that He had in prayer. In the Lord's Prayer, Jesus taught them to start by saying *"Our Father."* We are to see ourselves as children that can come to their father at any time or place. Our relationship with our biological fathers can affect the way we view God in prayer. God has given us the Holy Spirit to help us approach Him in prayer. The Holy Spirit fills us with love and helps us all to not only see God as our Father but also acknowledge Him as *"Father"* in prayer.

"For ye have not received the spirit of bondage again to fear; but ye have received the Spirit of adoption, whereby we cry, Abba, Father." (Romans 8:15)

The Holy Spirit helps us to know how to approach God and engage in different types of Prayer. There are different types of Prayer. We will briefly discuss Worship *(as a form of Prayer)*, Prayer of Consecration, Supplication, Intercession and Corporate Prayer.

Worship

We are created to worship God. We worship Him because He created us, He is Holy, He is Sovereign, He lives in us and without Him we are nothing. Your entire life should be a life of worship to God, not only when you sing to Him in worship. However, to access God's presence when we pray, the atmosphere we create matters to Him. God is Holy and enjoys the atmosphere created by us when we worship Him. Here is a description of worship in the throne room of God:

"10 The four and twenty elders fall down before him that sat on the throne, and worship him that liveth for ever and ever, and cast their crowns before the throne, saying, 11 Thou art worthy, O Lord, to receive glory and honour and power: for thou hast created all things, and for thy pleasure they are and were created." (Revelation 4:10-11)

Jesus was familiar with this type of heavenly worship since He lived there before coming here on earth. Jesus desires that we practice the activities of heaven on earth, as described in the Lord's Prayer, in Matthew 6:9-10:

"9 After this manner therefore pray ye: Our Father which art in heaven, Hallowed be thy name. 10 Thy kingdom come, Thy will be done in earth, as it is in heaven."

Jesus said *"Thy will be done on earth, as it is in heaven."* One of God's will for us is to worship Him. We are created to worship God. If we do not take time to worship God, we will worship something else which becomes our idol. God enjoys and responds to our worship. We can create an atmosphere of heaven here on earth through our worship with the help of the Holy Spirit. Jesus told the woman He met at the well about this type of worship. He said:

"God is a Spirit: and they that worship him must worship him in spirit and in truth." (John 4:24)

We worship in spirit and in truth with the help of the Holy Spirit which is God's desire for us all. We can partake of the heavenly worship in God's presence, as described in Revelations 4:8-11, only with the help of the Holy Spirit. We can worship in our understanding and in the Spirit by yielding ourselves to worship God in tongues.

Prayer of Consecration

This type of Prayer is when we deliberately create time to set ourselves apart to seek the face of God to know and follow His will. It is a form of *"Contemplative Prayer"* where we quietly reflect and wait to hear the voice of God.

There is so much noise and activity that bring distraction around us today. Periodically, we need to withdraw from the activities and noise of the Outer Court to be still in God's presence. It can happen when we first give our lives to Christ and any time we decide to re-focus on God during the course of our walk with Him. I did this when I gave first gave my life to Christ. I took time to have a personal retreat and asked God who I was in Him and He revealed it to me. It involves fasting with prayers focused on a particular request and waiting patiently for an answer.

"I waited patiently for the Lord; and he inclined unto me, and heard my cry." (Psalm 40:1)

Jesus made a prayer of consecration when He yielded to God's will for His life before His crucifixion:

"And he went a little farther, and fell on his face, and prayed, saying, O my Father, if it be possible, let this cup pass from me: nevertheless not as I will, but as thou wilt." (Matthew 26:39)

Prayer of Supplication

The Hebrew meaning of Supplication in the Bible is *"a Petition or a Request."* Prayer of Supplication is offered when we ask God for something like when we confess our sins, ask for forgiveness, give thanks for His numerous blessings and ask for things for ourselves. We should make it a habit to come to the Father in prayer by making daily confessions and asking for forgiveness of sins. It is important to note what Philippians 4:6 says *"Be careful for nothing; but in every thing by prayer and supplication with thanksgiving let your requests be made known unto God.*

Prayer of Intercession

To intercede means to *"intervene on behalf of another."* During prayer of intercession, others needs come first. We pray through a burden we have for others until God's will for that situation comes to pass. It is a selfless act and without any hidden motives. The intercessor rejoices when the request has been answered for others. Intercession usually involves putting on our spiritual armor and ready for spiritual warfare on behalf of others *(Ephesians 6:10-18)*. As believers, we are like soldiers on the battleground helping wounded soldiers and saving prisoners of war. It is important to note that engaging in spiritual warfare requires knowledge of the word of God and using it as the *"Sword of the Spirit"* to defeat the devil and his cohorts.

Corporate Prayer

As the word implies, corporate prayer involves praying together with other people whether in small groups like a family prayer meeting or larger bodies of people like in the church. These prayers are strategic and offered to God with a focus and to achieve a common goal.

The blessings and testimonies from corporate prayers are amazing. It is important to join a prayer group within your local church. It strengthens your prayer life especially when you do not feel like praying or when facing challenges that life may bring.

Praying in Private Tongues

Your private tongue is the prayer language you received when you experienced the Holy Spirit baptism. God gives everyone a unique language that can be used at will to communicate with Him. Isn't that awesome?

"For he that speaketh in an unknown tongue speaketh not unto men, but unto God: for no man understandeth him; howbeit in the spirit he speaketh mysteries." (1 Corinthians 14:2)

Praying in tongues builds up our faith in prayer and helps us pray more effectively to God.

"But ye, beloved, building up yourselves on your most holy faith, praying in the Holy Ghost." (Jude 1:20)

Many times, we have limited vocabulary in prayer. Private tongues help us pray effectively without ceasing *(1Thessalonians 5:16)*. It enhances our capacity to ask for things that we do not know about *(referred to as mysteries)* that will benefit our lives. Praying in tongues allow the

Holy Spirit to pray through us to God for the perfect solution for each situation in our lives.

"26 Likewise the Spirit also helpeth our infirmities: for we know not what we should pray for as we ought: but the Spirit itself maketh intercession for us with groanings which cannot be uttered. 27 And he that searcheth the hearts knoweth what is the mind of the Spirit, because he maketh intercession for the saints according to the will of God." *(Romans 8:26-27)*

Private tongues help us pray about the things that matter to God. It is not selfish prayer but the Holy Spirit prays through us when we yield our tongues in prayer. Many believers have stopped praying in tongues because they do not understand what they are saying or do not realize the potency of this gift. You can ask God for interpretation of your private tongues and He will reveal it to you.

"Wherefore let him that speaketh in an unknown tongue pray that he may interpret." *(1 Corinthians 14:13)*

Paul spent quality time praying in tongues and he taught the churches about the benefits of praying in tongues. He encouraged the church at Corinth to pray in tongues and in addition, to prophesy in order to build up the church.

"I would that ye all spake with tongues, but rather that ye prophesied: for greater is he that prophesieth than he that speaketh with tongues, except he interpret, that the church may receive edifying." (1 Corinthians 14:5)

Praying in tongues means your spirit bypasses your mind to communicate directly with God about your past, present and future *(1 Corinthians 14:2)*. The devil does not know what you are praying about. Private tongues give you more capacity to communicate with your heavenly Father in such a way that you would not have been able to express yourself. Your spirit *(the real you)* is presenting your burden to God on your behalf because your spirit knows what is best for you. Contrary to what people think, you have control over your private tongues. You can start and stop praying in tongues at your will. You can decide to pray in your understanding and can switch back to praying in tongues at will. Isn't that awesome?

"What is it then? I will pray with the spirit, and I will pray with the understanding also: I will sing with the spirit, and I will sing with the understanding also."
(1 Corinthians 14:15)

Also, praying in private tongues is linked to the operation of your unique spiritual gifts. Like Paul encouraged Timothy, I will encourage you to start praying in tongues and stir up the gifts God has placed within you.

"Wherefore I put thee in remembrance that thou stir up the gift of God, which is in thee by the putting on of my hands." (2 Timothy 1:6)

Journaling

It is a good habit to keep a journal. It helps you clear your mind and process your thoughts as you put them in a notebook. You are able to go back to the prayer points, ideas, thoughts and revelations written in your journal. You can write thoughts that come to your mind during bible study and after prayer. It is good practice to have a pen and journal by your bedside to document your ideas, thoughts, visions or dreams after rising up from bed. Daniel was a man who received multiple dreams and interpreted them. He could do this because he recorded them faithfully and went back to God in prayer about the visions and dreams he wrote down.

"In the first year of Belshazzar king of Babylon Daniel had a dream and visions of his head upon his bed: then he wrote the dream, and told the sum of the matters." (Daniel 7:1)

Journaling helps your prayer life. You can go back to God to thank Him when your prayer points are answered. God can reveal things to you that can enhance your prayer life just by keeping journals. I started journaling since I gave my life to Christ. It is amazing what I find I had written years ago while reviewing my journals.

"And the Lord answered me, and said, Write the vision, and make it plain upon tables, that he may run that readeth it."
(Habakkuk 2:2)

It is refreshing to see that today I am doing most of the things I wrote down many years ago when I gave my life to Christ. Writing your vision and mission statements, thoughts, ideas, goals, visions and dreams bring an inner excitement especially when they come to pass. People have written books, poems, hymns, songs, articles, and developed ideas into inventions from just journaling. Voice recorders can be used by those who prefer to vocalize their ideas which can be transcribed into text. We cannot always rely on our mind to keep track of the volume of information that is revealed to us daily. Statistics show that each person has about 70,000 thoughts per day *(48 thoughts per minute)*. Keeping a journal provides a central location and a reference point for happenings in our lives. We can refer to our journals to track patterns of events and have a better understanding of who we are.

Journaling shows God that we are being faithful stewards of the little He is revealing to us and He will give us more as we practice journaling. You can start by buying a pen and notepad and begin to write your thoughts. You will find out there is a lot within that you can express with your pen. Like the common saying *"A pen is mightier than a sword,"* so start journaling today!

CHAPTER 8

Trials

> *"Consider it pure joy, my brothers and*
> *sisters, whenever you face trials of many*
> *kinds." (James 1:2)*

Most Christians think that when they give their lives to Christ, all their trials will come to a permanent end. This thinking is false. I decided to discuss this topic in order for us to expect and embrace them. Trials are part of what shapes our identity. I experienced one barely two months after giving my life to Christ. Trials are not strangers to Christians and we should not be shocked when we go through them.

"Beloved, think it not strange concerning the fiery trial which is to try you, as though some strange thing happened unto you." (1 Peter 4:12)

Trials are not fun. However, God has designed them to be part of our spiritual journey. God tailors every trial for each of us with the purpose of getting the best out of us.

How we respond to trials matter to God. God desires that we receive trials with *"all joy"* which demands a paradigm shift in the way we view trials. Going to Six Flags is fun but suffering daily with illness, losing a business, or grief from any form of loss is not fun. How can we consider trials all joy when they surround us like a pride of roaring lions? Many have considered Christians as *"weak"* but we realize that *"enduring trials"* is not weak at all! Like the common saying *"What doesn't kill you only makes you stronger!"*

I believe that is why unbelievers are unable to comprehend how Christians endure trials. When we apply this principle of having a *"joyful countenance"* to situations in life, it goes contrary to the norm and we may be perceived as being simply in gross denial. Sometimes, we feel alone and find it quite difficult to even open our mouths to pray. The Holy Spirit is ever present to comfort and strengthen us through trials. We can do all things through Christ who strengthens us *(Philippians 4:13).*

Having a *"joyful attitude"* does not mean that we deny the fact that there is a real tough battle. As stated in 1 Peter 5:10, we are rest assured that every trial has a time limit and the end result takes us to the next level in Christ:

"But the God of all grace, who hath called us unto his eternal glory by Christ Jesus, after that ye have suffered a while, make you perfect, stablish, strengthen, settle you."

We have to embrace the fact that there will always be trials. We do not pray for them to happen but when they do, we welcome trials as we will welcome a friend we have not seen in a long time. If we happen to meet an old friend that we have not seen for many years, how will we react? Our faces are not sad when we see them. We will not welcome them with a disgruntled attitude. We will open our hearts to them and receive them with joy just as James said.

James 1:2 tells us not to welcome trials simply with joy, but to welcome them with "*all joy.*" This is quite hard to comprehend but God knows His grace is sufficient for us *(2 Corinthians 12:9)*. God knows that we are able to bear whatever He allows to come our way. We are not to despise this period but learn from it. All that we experience during trials work together for our good as they help us grow spiritually *(Romans 8:28)*. Trials are designed to make us spiritually mature and help us be more like Christ. We should receive trials in our lives with all joy and endure them.

"Thou therefore endure hardness, as a good soldier of Jesus Christ." (2 Timothy 2:3)

We are being tested so that we might look more like Christ in terms of patience and endurance. We are being tested so that we might become mature and complete, with a pure and undefiled faith. We go through testing so that we learn patience which is the key to contentment and receiving God's best at the time He has for us.

"3 Knowing this, that the trying of your faith worketh patience. 4 But let patience have her perfect work, that ye may be perfect and entire, wanting nothing."
(James 1:3-4)

If we deeply want to grow in Christ and enjoy greater intimacy with Him, we should persevere through trials with a joyful countenance. They may cut deep, but it is a light affliction that lasts for a moment and in the end, we become much more Christ-like Christians. *(2 Corinthians 4:17).* The Eagle loves the storm. It is the only bird that uses the currents from the storm to soar high above the clouds without flapping its wings. It just soars to greater heights on the current of the storm. Like the eagle, we come out of trials more refined, with great testimonies, stronger in faith and having a better appreciation of our relationship with God.

If we deeply want to grow in Christ and enjoy greater intimacy with Him, we should persevere through trials with a joyful countenance.

There is a second reality that empowers us toward rejoicing and having joy in the midst of trials. We note that if we are being tested, then there must be someone giving the test. We know that we are not suffering in vain but for Christ Himself. God has designed the particular trial. He will carry us and see us through it all. If you know Christ and you are passing through the fire today, consider it all joy. Welcome the various and diverse trials as old friends. It is Christ Himself who is working out His great plan in your life knowing that nothing can separate you from His love.

"Who shall separate us from the love of Christ? shall tribulation, or distress, or persecution, or famine, or nakedness, or peril, or sword?" (Romans 8:35)

The account of Job's trials will cause us to appreciate the level and extent of God's love for us. No one will like to experience what Job experienced. Job was a man who lost everything in life through trials and he came out of the trial way better than he was originally. Trials strengthen our relationship with God. It changes the way we view and relate with Him.

"I have heard of thee by the hearing of the ear: but now mine eye seeth thee." (Job 42:5)

Most people observe that their intimacy with God during trials is or was at a higher and greater level. Trials cause us to leave everything we hold dear to focus our attention on God for help. God's plan is not to have us experience trials all the time in order to enjoy intimacy with Him. God wants us to have intimacy with Him at all times. However, God gets more of our attention when we go through trials.

Just a few months after giving my life to Christ, I shared in Chapter 3 that I lost my Dad. I had a great relationship with my Dad and I strongly believe that God saved me and prepared me before his death for a reason. God knew that I will not have been able to handle my Dad's death without Him. I received great comfort from the word of God through it all. I remember God's soothing words reminding me that He created my Dad and that He loved me even more than the way my Dad loved me. I know God as my Father now since I read that He is the Father of the Fatherless. As I mentioned earlier, one of the words that I received which gave me great comfort and strength through it all was Isaiah 48:10-11:

"10 Behold, I have refined thee, but not with silver; I have chosen thee in the furnace of affliction. 11 For mine own sake, even for mine own sake, will I do it: for how should my name be polluted? and I will not give my glory unto another."

God is only working spiritual fruit in us so that we might become mature and complete and in turn be like

Him and enjoy Him more intimately. Trials do to believers what the furnace does to mineral ore in the production of precious metals like Gold, Silver and Platinum. Trials, like the furnace help to refine us at every stage to conform us to the character of Jesus Christ. The furnace brings out all the impurities from the excavated rocks containing the minerals to be refined. The heat of the furnace is turned up until impurities rise to the surface to reveal gold, silver or platinum. They can be called *"Precious Metals"* only after going through the fiery furnace. Like the furnace, trials are designed to bring out all our impurities and make us more precious to behold after coming out of them.

"He will be like a refiner and purifier of silver; He will purify the sons of Levi and refine them like gold and silver. Then they will present offerings to the LORD in righteousness." (Malachi 3:3)

Every woman that has gone through labor knows the pain of childbirth. The bible references a woman's *"joy"* after childbirth which cannot compare to the pain she endured during labor. Trials are like labor pains. We come out of them more refined than we were before the trial.

"A woman when she is in travail hath sorrow, because her hour is come: but as soon as she is delivered of the child, she remembereth no more the anguish, for joy that a man is born into the world." (John 16:21)

Trials come in cycles and are part of what makes us who we are as believers. We could be experiencing a trial, coming out of one or going into one right now. We should expect them and welcome them with joy. Jesus was not exempt from trials. He endured numerous trials while here on earth. Jesus knew what it was to be rejected by people from His country when He said in Luke 4:24, "*... Verily I say unto you, No prophet is accepted in his own country.*"

He knew what it felt like to go through trials alone and feel forsaken. He was falsely accused, flogged and crucified, yet prayed that God should forgive them for their actions because they did not know what they were doing. Matthew 27:46 says "*And about the ninth hour Jesus cried with a loud voice, saying, Eli, Eli, lama sabachthani? that is to say, My God, my God, why hast thou forsaken me?*"

Jesus was tested and prevailed in every trial He faced as noted in Hebrews 4:15, "*For we have not an high priest which cannot be touched with the feeling of our infirmities; but was in all points tempted like as we are, yet without sin.*" Jesus knew that He would be nailed to the cross, yet He endured it for the joy of our salvation. Always rejoice in trials and your time of rejoicing will surely come. Psalm 30:5 says "*...weeping may endure for a night, but joy cometh in the morning.*" May God strengthen you in all trials.

CHAPTER 9

The Church and I

*"The Church is a body of believers that
fellowship together, shares each other's
burden and care for one another."*

What is the first thing that comes to mind
when you hear the word *"Church"*? It means
different things to different people.
However, one major thought is that the church is a
building. The word *"Church"* originates from the Greek
word meaning *"an assembly."* The root meaning of church
is not that of a building, but of *"People."* It is quite
interesting to know that when asked what church people
attend, most people describe a building. The church was
birth by the Holy Spirit on the day of Pentecost. It
comprised of those who waited for and experienced the
power of the Holy Spirit as described in Acts Chapter 2
and commonly referred to as the *"Early Church."*

"1 And when the day of Pentecost was fully come, they were all with one accord in one place. 2 And suddenly there came a sound from heaven as of a rushing mighty wind, and it filled all the house where they were sitting. 3 And there appeared unto them cloven tongues like as of fire, and it sat upon each of them. 4 And they were all filled with the Holy Ghost, and began to speak with other tongues, as the Spirit gave them utterance." (Acts 2:1-4)

The church plays an important role in the life of every believer. The church is a body of believers that fellowship together, share each other's burden and care for one another.

"And they continued stedfastly in the apostles' doctrine and fellowship, and in breaking of bread, and in prayers." (Acts 2:42)

The church is where we serve our God given gifts, skills and talents in such a way that God's name is glorified. God is able to manifest His grace through us.

"As every man hath received the gift, even so minister the same one to another, as good stewards of the manifold grace of God." (1 Peter 4:10)

We are to prayerfully ask God where to serve our gifts in the church to benefit everyone. Our service to God should be birth from our intimate relationship with Him. I prayed earnestly to God about where He wanted me to serve and where I would be most effective before deciding to serve. I waited a year while praying and studying the word before serving in my local church.

> *Our service to God should be birth from our intimate relationship with Him.*

"In all thy ways acknowledge him, and he shall direct thy paths." (Proverbs 3:6)

It is very important to patiently seek the face of the Lord before deciding where to plug into the church to serve. Pressure from friends or family members to serve where they serve can eventually lead to eye-service, frustration, incompetency and burnout. You have to put into consideration your passion, skills and spiritual gifts in relation to the area you will like to serve. It will be a rewarding experience in the long term for you, your team members and also those you will be serving.

"Not slothful in business; fervent in spirit; serving the Lord." (Romans 12:11)

Our true identity in Christ will compel us to bless others by serving them with all that we are. Our true identity is not selfish but service driven. Jesus Christ did not desire any reputation or title here on earth but to fulfil His assignment. Our true identity compels us to replace our ambition with God's vision and purpose. God helps us live a life contrary to what we have known. Jesus Christ made a critical statement about service to His disciples.

"26 But it shall not be so among you: but whosoever will be great among you, let him be your minister; 27 And whosoever will be chief among you, let him be your servant: 28 Even as the Son of man came not to be ministered unto, but to minister, and to give his life a ransom for many." (Matthew 20:26-28)

Understanding the Fivefold Ministry

Having an understanding of the fivefold ministry and how each office relates to your calling and service to God is important. The operation of the fivefold ministry has not been fully executed. The offices of the fivefold ministry are listed in *verse 11* of the scripture below:

*"11 And he gave some, **apostles**; and some, **prophets**; and some, **evangelists**; and some, **pastors** and **teachers**; 12 For*

the perfecting of the saints, for the work of the ministry, for the edifying of the body of Christ: 13 Till we all come in the unity of the faith, and of the knowledge of the Son of God, unto a perfect man, unto the measure of the stature of the fulness of Christ." (Ephesians 4:11-13)

"And God hath set some in the church, first apostles, secondarily prophets, thirdly teachers, after that miracles, then gifts of healings, helps, governments, diversities of tongues." (1 Corinthians 12:28)

God established these offices to work together in unity in order to achieve common kingdom goals *(Psalm 133:1-2)*. However, the most profiled and desired office is that of the Pastor. They are faced with lots of pressure due to the demand placed on the office. The ministerial work is meant to be spread across the five offices for the common goal of soul winning, spreading the gospel and building God's kingdom. God has equipped us to function as a body but the church is not fully operating in this manner. The office of the Pastor is just one of the five offices God has established for the church. Isn't it is easier to pick up a dumbbell with five fingers of the hand than to use a finger?

*"And it came to pass at the seventh time, that he said, Behold, there ariseth a little cloud out of the sea, **like a***

man's hand. *And he said, Go up, say unto Ahab, Prepare thy chariot, and get thee down that the rain stop thee not."* (1 Kings 18:44)

As described in the scripture above, Elijah's servant saw a cloud that looked like a man's hand (*with five fingers representing the fivefold ministry*). He saw a cloud in form of a hand rise which represents the fivefold church that will produce the rain necessary for the great harvest of souls. The church (*assembly of believers*) will move into the coming revival and walk in authority in this end time. Believers will seek to know who they are in Christ and begin to walk in the revelation of that knowledge as a body. God's hand will raise the church into the place of authority once the fivefold ministry is fully recognized and operational.

The amazing aspect of the fivefold ministry is that each office can operate and function in any church in the world in the body of Christ. You can go to any church in the world and function in your divine office. The fivefold ministry can be explained using the fingers of the hand to represent each office. It is important to know that it is the Holy Spirit who reveals what office we are called to operate in. God can reveal our office to us if we ask in prayer and others will be able to confirm it over time. Your office is part of your divine identity in Christ.

Fivefold Ministry
The office of the Apostle – (*The Thumb*)

The thumb represents the "*Apostle*" who helps to restore order and unity in churches, establish churches or ministry related programs, and identify the ministry gifts in others. Apostles ensure that the foundations of churches are built on the proper spiritual principles and doctrines. Apostles are church planters and nurture the growth of startup churches.

The office of the Prophet – (*The Index Finger*)

The index finger represents the "*Prophet*" which is referred to as the "*Pointer Finger*". The Prophet speaks the mind of God in situations bringing revelation, guidance, instruction, correction or judgment to the body of Christ. The office of the prophet differs from the gift of prophecy. The Prophet brings a word or message from God. However, according to 1 Corinthians 14:3, the gift of prophecy is for edification, exhortation and comfort. It is important to note that not everyone who prophesies is a prophet but an individual who operates from the office of a prophet can prophesy. Like Apostles, Prophets are able to recognize God's gifts and callings on others.

The office of the Evangelist – (*The Middle Finger*)

The middle finger represents the "*Evangelist.*" The middle finger is the longest of the fingers on the hand which represents the outreach ministry. An evangelist has oversight over evangelism and outreach programs. They champion most of the soul winning aspects of the church and focus most of their time and energy on ways to spread the gospel to people outside the local church. Evangelists have an ability to touch hardened hearts with God's love in order for them to receive salvation.

The office of the Pastor – (*The Ring Finger*)

The ring finger represents the "*Pastor,*" hence the Pastor's dedication to the church members. Pastors are shepherd-like in their relationship with the church members. Pastors are actively involved in the welfare of their church members such as birthdays, baby dedication, weddings, funerals, hospital visits, prayer, spiritual counseling, and other such pastoral responsibilities. Pastors are nurturers and lay down their lives for the flock. They try not to give up on people because they have a large heart.

The office of the Teacher – (*The Little Finger*)

The little finger represents the *"Teacher"*. The office of Teacher is one that stirs others to know and seek the truth. The Teacher provides balance and truth through instruction in the principles of the word of God. Teachers love truth and love to study. They love to write, read and study various topics that enhance their teaching ability. Teachers usually have oversight over the training and educational ministries of the church including developing curriculum and performing teaching duties such as Sunday School, Baptismal Classes, and so on. Teachers love to dig deep when they study before giving any new insight or revelation and stay far away from heresy or doctrinal error.

As mentioned earlier in Ephesians 4:12, one of the goals of the fivefold ministry is to perfect the saints through discipleship for the work of the ministry and to edify the body of Christ. We are supposed to continue to experience spiritual growth through discipleship in the local church.

The church is a safe haven and platform to express and sharpen our gifts, skills and talents without fear and prejudice just as Proverbs 27:17 says *"Iron sharpeneth iron; so a man sharpeneth the countenance of his friend."*

All corrections in the use of our gifts, skills and talents are to be done in love, bearing in mind that we are all being prepared to serve our gifts to the world.

"But speaking the truth in love, may grow up into him in all things, which is the head, even Christ." *(Ephesians 4:15)*

Do you see yourself already operating in any one of these offices or feel a particular affinity for any one of them? Whether no or yes, you have to prayerfully seek the face of God to reveal to you more about your office.

"Before I formed thee in the belly I knew thee; and before thou camest forth out of the womb I sanctified thee, and I ordained thee a prophet unto the nations." (Jeremiah 1:5)

From this scripture, God hints us that He has divinely assigned an office to everyone even before we were formed in the womb. God told Jeremiah that he was a prophet. You know little about who you really are until you ask God in the Holy of Holies. You may be next great Apostle, Prophet, Evangelist, Pastor or Teacher that God plans to use to be a blessing to your generation. The world is waiting for you, so ask God about your true identity today!

CHAPTER 10

Exploits!

"For the earnest expectation of the
creature waiteth for the manifestation of
the sons of God." Romans 8:19

Are you ready to do exploits? The whole world is also waiting for you to display God's power and love which are the two major virtues from our identity in Christ. Romans 8:19 clearly tells us that the whole world is waiting for us not only to discover who we are in Christ but to also demonstrate the power that comes from knowing who we truly are. This clearly sums up the *"Great Commission"* that Jesus declared to His disciples and His expectation from every believer.

"15 And he said unto them, Go ye into all the world, and preach the gospel to every creature. 16 He that believeth and is baptized shall be saved; but he that believeth not shall be damned." (Mark 16:15-16)

We have been through the journey from the Outer Court to the Holies of Holies! The Holies of Holies is where we are told who we are and receive instruction about what to do with who we are. It was in here that Elijah received the word of God that he brought to King Ahab in 1 Kings 18:15a, *"And Elijah said, As the LORD of hosts liveth, before whom I stand."* The Ark of the Covenant and the Mercy Seat are located here. This is where God resides and the angels surround His presence. We experience lots of angelic activity, God's mercy, grace and glory in here.

Today, the Holies of Holies also referred to as the *"Secret Place"* or *"Throne Room"* is where we obtain mercy when we come before God in prayer and supplication. It is the place where we hear the heartbeat of God and experience His presence like Adam and Eve in the Garden of Eden. It is the place where we are moved with compassion to do His will just like the prophets in the Old Testament such as Jeremiah, Isaiah, and Ezekiel who encountered God and surrendered to His will.

Jesus prayed from the Holies of Holies, when He said *"Not my will but Your will be done" (Luke 22:42).* It is a place of surrender. It is a place where all our selfish ambition dies and we decide to live for Christ. It is the place of rest which is our *"Spiritual Promise Land."* It is a place where we cease from our works and yield to God. It is the place where we deliberately shut out every noise to become still in order to know God *(Psalm 46:10)*. It is this secret place where we are meant to abide *(Psalm 91:1-2)* and begin to enjoy the blessings of abiding in God's presence as mentioned in Psalm 91:3-16.

"1 He that dwelleth in the secret place of the most High shall abide under the shadow of the Almighty. 2 I will say of the Lord, He is my refuge and my fortress: my God; in him will I trust." (Psalm 91:1-2)

It is the place where Moses saw God face to face and his face shone *(Exodus 34:35)* or where we see Jesus and say *"Behold the Lamb of God" (John 1:29)*. It is the place the bible refers to as *"Heavenly Places"* in Christ Jesus.

"And hath raised us up together, and made us sit together in heavenly places in Christ Jesus." (Ephesians 2:6)

Paul mentioned that we are to get rid of every fear in our lives. We cannot do this on our own. As mentioned in Chapter 2, fear is from our fallen nature. It is a by-product of pride and rebellion. It brings with it low self-esteem and inferiority complex. We can only be redeemed and restored to our original state by the power and love received from the Holy Spirit. We have the promise of the Spirit because Jesus died on the cross making the Holy Spirit available to all.

"For God hath not given us the spirit of fear; but of power, and of love, and of a sound mind." (2 Timothy 1:7)

This scripture sums up our true identity in Christ. It is important to note that the Holy Spirit brings three major divine attributes into our lives that help us be like Christ. These attributes are Love, Power and Sound Mind. Love refers to the fruit of the Spirit. Power refers to the gifts of the Spirit and the office *(which is the fivefold ministry)* we operate in. Sound Mind refers to our capacity to reason and make the right decision or judgement. We have discussed the spiritual offices in Chapter 9, so we will discuss the gifts and fruit of the spirit in this chapter.

Gifts of the Spirit

The Holies of Holies is the place where we are imparted with the gifts of the Spirit and begin to operate fully in them. The world is waiting for those who will consecrate themselves to God to enjoy the secret place for the sake of operating in the fullness of His Spirit. The level of the operation of these gifts is determined by our consecration to God. God gives His gifts to those who ask and desire them with their whole heart.

"If ye then, being evil, know how to give good gifts unto your children: how much more shall your heavenly Father give the Holy Spirit to them that ask him?" (Luke 11:13)

It is important to note that God's gifts and calling are irrevocable so we have to ensure that we live a consecrated lifestyle to remain intimate with Him.

"For the gifts and calling of God are without repentance." (Romans 11:29)

As we serve our gifts in the church we have to remember that all God will put in us is not only for the church but for the world. As mentioned earlier, the church has a role for every believer. It is the place of fellowship and a safe platform to express our gifts with the goal of preparing us for the world. There are people in the world who are sick and distressed that will only receive their healing or deliverance when they encounter our newly discovered identity in God *(Romans 8:19)*.

Jesus mentioned that we are the light of the word. He has placed gifts in us that are meant to make us shine and relevant, not only in the church but to the world.

"14 Ye are the light of the world. A city that is set on an hill cannot be hid. 15 Neither do men light a candle, and put it under a bushel, but on a candlestick; and it giveth light unto all that are in the house." (Matthew 5:14-15)

I remember growing up, my cousin who was about ten years old at that time, came to stay with us for a couple of weeks. One afternoon, we could not find him. We became frantic since he was visiting and unfamiliar with the area. After searching for hours, we were astonished to find him fast asleep and sweating profusely under the bed. He had fallen off the bed and had rolled under it while still asleep. Sweet dreams, huh?

We are compared to salt that makes food tasteful. We are to bring flavor to the world with our spiritual gifts.

Our gifts may be asleep, hidden away like my cousin under the bed. We are to search for it, find it and then light it up for the world to see. Everyone has their unique gift(s). We are like a Christmas tree with gifts placed beneath it waiting to be unwrapped. It is our responsibility to unwrap the gift(s) though God has placed them within us. We are not meant to hide our gift(s). Also, the bible says we are the *"Salt of the Earth"* (Matthew 5:13).

We are compared to salt that makes food tasteful. We are to bring flavor to the world with our spiritual gifts.

As believers, the church can become a bushel where our light can become hidden, if we do not operate in them. If we read about the story of David, he was a warrior who had mighty men but they hid in a cave called Adullam.

"Now three of the thirty captains went down to the rock to David, into the cave of Adullam; and the host of the Philistines encamped in the valley of Rephaim."
(1 Chronicles 11:15)

The church can be like the cave of Adullam filled with believers who enjoy the comfort of refuge without displaying their gifts to the world. We are responsible and accountable for the gifts given to us. Jesus mentioned this to His disciples in the parable of the talents *(Matthew 25:14-30)*.

The church can be compared to a pregnant woman whose child enjoys the comfort of the womb and refuses to come out after nine months. Every believer has a spiritual life cycle in the womb of the church. It begins when we give our lives to Christ until when we are ready to serve our gift(s) to the world. However, we can enjoy the comfort of the church for many years and refuse to come out into the world to serve our gift(s). The world is in turmoil and distress waiting for believers to bring relief with our God-given office and gifts.

"For the earnest expectation of the creature waiteth for the manifestation of the sons of God." (Romans 8:19)

Jesus was *"the church"* to the disciples when He was here on earth. He used Himself as the platform to prepare them for the world. Jesus told them many parables that indicated that His time with them was going to be short. Jesus ascended into heaven after His death, and they realized that they were going into the world to do the *"greater works"* he frequently spoke about with the help of the Holy Spirit, who He promised will come.

Jesus told His disciples to wait for power from heaven that they will need to do exploits. It is out of the union of our spirit with the Holy Spirit and the capacity of power that our spirit can retain that the power of the Holy Spirit flows for us to do His work. Daniel said *"those that know their God shall be strong and they shall do exploits"* *(Daniel 11:32)*. Our spirit is like the vessel or plumb line that the power of God flows through to do His work.

"He that believeth on me, as the scripture hath said, out of his belly shall flow rivers of living water." (John 7:38)

If you grew up watching cartoons, reading comics, and even sketching your favorite Superhero on the back of your notebooks *(which I did)*, the idea of men, women or kids having supernatural or superhuman powers will not be strange to you. They are fictional characters who fight crime, protect and save their cities from supervillains. X-men had gifted mutants *(like Storm, Wolverine, Cyclops, Professor X)* with varying power and abilities, Superman had an indestructible body and his X-ray Vision, Flash moves at the speed of lightning, Thor has his indestructible hammer, Spiderman has spider senses and a strong web, Batman has physical strength and detective skills, Captain America has an indestructible shield and Hulk has incredible strength.

Like our encounter with the Holy Spirit during water baptism and Holy Spirit baptism, these Superheroes at one point had an encounter with something greater than them. After their encounter, they learnt more about their unique super powers and had to come to terms with them. They began to discover that their superhuman abilities were given not for their selfish ambition but to protect their city or country from danger. One common trait, I observe about Superheroes is that at some point, they had an identity crisis and they eventually had to accept their new identity after their encounter. They realized that they possessed supernatural abilities because their assignment was greater than them. Spiderman named *"Peter Parker"* was a teenager in High School. After he had an encounter at a public science exhibition, he discovered he possessed supernatural abilities. Peter Parker is known to quote one of his late Uncle's final words to him:

"With great power comes great responsibility."
– Uncle Ben to Peter Parker (Spiderman)

The Superheroes of X-Men were quite different. They were born with superhuman abilities and referred to as *"Mutants."* A man named Charles Xavier, *(also known as Professor X)* created a school for gifted mutants to train and develop their gifts. The people of the city discriminated against the mutants because of their superhuman abilities. However, Professor X helped them build their confidence and they eventually accepted who they were as mutants. They began to operate boldly in their unique gifts to save the residents of the city from the evil villain, Magneto. Magneto is a mutant who went rogue and wanted to destroy humans because of the resident's hatred for mutants. Professor X had a burden to help these gifted mutants and he made a profound statement about them:

"A new generation of mutants is emerging, that much is certain. They will be called freaks, genetic monstrosities. But they are emerging in the inner cities, in the suburbs, in the deserts and the jungles. And when they emerge, they will need teachers; people who can help them overcome their anger and show them how to use their strange gifts responsibly. They will need us." – Professor X (Earth-616)

This sums up our affinity for Superheroes and why we aspire to have unique powers and abilities. This innate desire is from our spirit man longing to experience the supernatural. What Professor X is to the mutants is what the Holy Spirit is to us. A new generation of believers is emerging who will totally yield to the leading of the Holy Spirit to do great exploits for the kingdom of God. The Holy Spirit desires to teach every believer how to discover who they are in Christ and release the power within them to benefit all. He teaches us to be responsible with all that we have been given from our heavenly Father so that His name may be glorified.

There are nine supernatural gifts of the Spirit that we can receive from God and serve to the world, as mentioned in 1 Corinthians 12:7-11:

"7 But the manifestation of the Spirit is given to every man to profit withal. 8 For to one is given by the Spirit the word of wisdom; to another the word of knowledge by the same Spirit; 9 To another faith by the same Spirit; to another the gifts of healing by the same Spirit; 10 To another the working of miracles; to another prophecy; to another discerning of spirits; to another divers kinds of tongues; to another the interpretation of tongues: 11 But all these worketh that one and the selfsame Spirit, dividing to every man severally as he will."

We will briefly describe the nine gifts of the spirit which are received supernaturally from God by the Holy Spirit:

- The gift of the **word of wisdom** is the supernatural ability to give guidance or offer a solution to a complex situation with knowledge from the present or from the future.

- The gift of the **word of knowledge** is the supernatural ability to give guidance or offer a solution to a complex situation with knowledge from the past or present.

- The *gift of **discerning of spirits*** is the ability to decipher whether a message, event or person, or situation is from God or the devil.

- The *gift of **divers kinds of tongues*** is the ability to speak in a foreign language *(that you did not know how to speak)* in order to communicate the gospel message to someone who speaks the language.

- The *gift of **prophecy*** is the ability to bring the message of God for a particular situation. The message from God will usually strengthen, encourage and comfort the hearers. For this reason, Paul admonishes us to desire spiritual gifts, especially the gift of prophecy.

- The *gift of **interpretation of tongues*** is the ability to translate the tongues other people are speaking and communicate it back in your own language for everyone to understand.

- The *gift of **faith*** is the ability to believe or trust God for the impossible no matter how difficult the situation may be.

- The *gift of **healing*** is the ability to use God's healing power to heal the sick and all manners of diseases which may involve casting out demons.

- The *gift **working of miracles*** is the ability to perform signs and wonders that validate the word of God.

For easy understanding of the operations of the gifts, they can be grouped into three categories:

1. Revelation Gifts *(Word of Wisdom, Word of Knowledge and Discerning of Spirits)*
2. Vocal *Gifts (Prophesy, Divers kinds of Tongues and Interpretation of Tongues)*
3. Power Gifts *(Faith, Healing and Working of Miracles)*

You are to serve your gift(s) according to the grace of the spiritual office *(Fivefold Ministry)* that God has given you. It is the Holy Spirit who distributes these gifts according to the grace God gives each believer who asks wholeheartedly. You will be like *"fish in water"* when you operate within the grace that God has given you.

"6 Having then gifts differing according to the grace that is given to us, whether prophecy, let us prophesy according to the proportion of faith." (Romans 12:6)

Fruit of the Spirit

It is important to note that love is the foundation and litmus test for the full operation of the gifts of the Spirit. All that we do has to be done in love. As we know,

God is love so is Jesus and the Holy Spirit. Love is described powerfully in 1 Corinthians 13. It sums up love as the greatest virtue to have. There is no law that can be written against anyone who displays God's love. Love conquers all the gifts and virtues that we may desire to have. The final verse in the chapter says *"And now abideth faith, hope, charity, these three; but the greatest of these is charity."* *(Kindly note that Charity means Love)*

There are nine fruit of the Spirit as mentioned in Galatians 5:22-23 which are listed below:

"22 But the fruit of the Spirit is love, joy, peace, longsuffering, gentleness, goodness, faith, 23 Meekness, temperance: against such there is no law."

Our motives come into play here. God knows and sees our heart so we cannot deceive Him. The operation of the gifts is rooted in love and it can be hindered by pride or any selfish motives in our heart. The purpose of the gift of the Spirit is to benefit everyone and not just ourselves.

"But Peter said unto him, Thy money perish with thee, because thou hast thought that the gift of God may be purchased with money." *(Acts 8:20)*

God wants us to bear the fruit of the Spirit because they reflect His divine character. Our spiritual maturity is measured based on how much of these fruit we bear as we grow daily in Christ. We cannot bear the fruit of the Spirit on our own which is why we need the Holy Spirit to help us with each one of them. We can briefly go over the meaning of each fruit.

Love is not just an emotion. One of the ways to show love is to put our gifts to action. God is love and all that He does is based on His love for us. Love is the character of God which He desires that we emulate. God gave up His son, Jesus for us. This type of Love is called *"Agape or Unconditional Love."* As it simply implies, love without conditions or motives. God can help us love others the way He does.

Joy can be easily mistaken for happiness. Happiness like Joy is the same feeling we express when we buy a house or car, get into High School or College, get married or promoted. However, the difference is that the source of our joy is from the indwelling presence of the Holy Spirit and Happiness is from an external source. For this reason, we say *"The joy of the Lord is our strength."*

Peace is that unexplainable calmness we have within even in the midst of crisis. We have this peace because we know God has control of the situation. Jesus is the *"Prince of*

Peace. "We get our peace from Him through meditating on the words in the Bible and by focusing on God in prayer.

Longsuffering goes much further than patience. It is giving room for God to act on our behalf and waiting calmly for an answer that can take months or years to be answered.

Gentleness is being mindful of the feelings of others and their emotions at all times. It involves the way we treat others in every situation. We may have heard believers say *"The Holy Spirit is a Gentleman"* because even though we sin, He gently corrects us.

Goodness is doing the right thing at all times in every situation. It involves looking for the best interest of others without partiality in any situation whether it is in our favor or not. The goodness in us will seek to overcome every trace of evil that may be intended to hurt or harm others.

Faith is being steadfast, trustworthy and loyal in our dealings with others and with God. It involves being reliable and having a great sense of commitment in every situation we that may find ourselves.

Meekness goes beyond humility and gentleness. It is a virtue that helps us to be mindful that we possess the power of God for a divine purpose. Knowing this, meekness restrains us and keeps us from abusing God's power.

Temperance means controlling ourselves. Without the Holy Spirit we can do some wild things. His presence in our lives helps us to control our desires and passions. Self-Control involves keeping ourselves from doing things that displeases God. God desires that we are in control of the things we do in order to live a life that honors Him.

It is important to note that we cannot produce these virtues by ourselves. We need God's help to bear the fruit of the Spirit. From studying the word of God, we realize that these are not *"fruits of the Spirit"* but the *"fruit of the Spirit"* with nine qualities or virtues. The more we seek God to be like Jesus the more the Holy Spirit helps us to bear much more fruit. I pray that you will bear much fruit as you seek Him.

May God bless you on your journey of self-discovery in Christ. I pray that this book will serve as a catalyst to stir up your pursuit of God. May God grant you the grace to live a life full of purpose and impact leaving a great legacy for many generations to come in Jesus name.

Connect with

Toks

Facebook

www.facebook.com/inspiredscripts

Twitter

www.twitter.com/inspiredscripts

Instagram

www.instagram.com/inspiredscripts

Web

www.inspiredscripts.org

www.toksakinsanmi.com

Email

toks@inspiredscripts.org

info@toksakinsanmi.com

62845173R00098

Made in the USA
Columbia, SC
06 July 2019